LIVING WITH
THE ENEMY

£5

To Alex

With my very

best wishes

20/01/2012

D1580743

FREDDIE KNOLLER
WITH JOHN LANDAW

LIVING WITH THE ENEMY

MY SECRET LIFE ON THE RUN FROM THE NAZIS

metro

Published by Metro Publishing Ltd,
3, Bramber Court, 2 Bramber Road,
London W14 9PB, England

www.johnblakepublishing.co.uk

First published in paperback in 2005

ISBN 978 1 84358 142 0

British Library Cataloguing-in-Publication Data:

A catalogue record for this book is available from the British Library.

Design by www.envydesign.co.uk

Printed in Great Britain by
CPI Antony Rowe, Chippenham, Wiltshire

5 7 9 10 8 6

Contents

Acknowledgements

FIRST OF all I must thank my daughters, Marcia and Susie. Without their insistence on that Friday night so many years ago that I tell them my story this book may never have been written. Instead I would have remained silent and been condemned to relive the terrors of the war years in the nightmares which plagued me.

I am for ever grateful to my darling wife, Freda, who has had to live with the consequences of that evening – my obsession with the Holocaust. This book has been in preparation for five years and, though I know I have sorely tried her patience, she has supported me throughout.

I would like to thank my dear friend and fellow survivor Leo Bretholz, who mentions our friendship in his book *Leap into Darkness*, and who encouraged me to write this book.

I shall always be indebted to my late sister-in-law, Vivian, and her daughter, Janice, for providing me with all the letters written by my parents to my late brother, Eric.

My brother Otto and his wife, Lotte, deserve my special gratitude for reminding me of events long forgotten. In that context I am also grateful to my cousins Rosi Schächter and Maxl Bodek for answering so many questions about our lives together as refugees in Belgium and France.

I wish to thank many people for their support, assistance and encouragement. I am for ever indebted to my good friend and co-author John Landaw, who brought to bear his skills as a writer to shape this book, and his training as a lawyer and psychotherapist to draw from me the many memories, some painful, necessary to convey just what it was really like being a refugee Jew in those dark days. I should also thank Ernest Lewin, Drusilla Redman, Ann Kritzinger and Lauren Parker, who read the manuscript and made many helpful suggestions, and Simon Reiss, who suggested the title of the book.

I owe a particular debt of gratitude to Mary Remnant, who gave freely and unstintingly of her professional time in helping to edit the book, and to Gilbert Fouquet, who has translated the book into French.

For her continual encouragement and support I am deeply grateful to my dear friend Susi Bradfield, and indeed to the whole Bradfield–Brett family.

To Sir Martin Gilbert, who has included an extract of my story in his book *Never Again*, I owe a special debt of gratitude for his endorsement of mine.

I would also like to thank my very good friend Alan Symons for his counsel and encouragement. Because of his untimely death, he was not able to see the final version of my book or this acknowledgement.

Without the help of several organisations and the individuals in them I would have been seriously hampered in my preparation of the book.

My thanks go to Judith Hassan, Rachelle Lazarus and Melanie Gotlieb of the Holocaust Survivors Centre in London.

Suzanne Bardgett, Director of the Holocaust Exhibition at the Imperial War Museum in London, has encouraged me to write my story and has kindly offered to hold the book launch at the Museum.

My sincere thanks go to Danny Elkanati, Dr Henry Stellman and Florrie Raymond of State of Israel Bonds for arranging a further book launch for their clients in the UK.

I am deeply grateful to my diligent and gifted editor, Richard Dawes.

Last, but certainly not least, I am indebted to my very good friend Dr Elisabeth Maxwell, of Remembering for the Future 2000, who has helped me so much with advice, contacts and encouragement. Thank you, Betty.

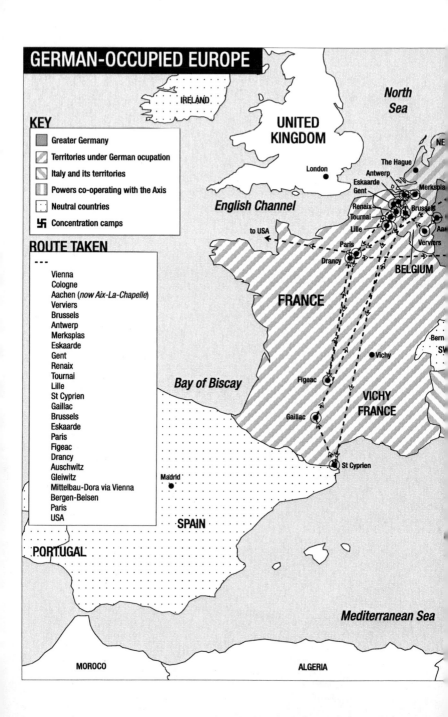

GERMAN-OCCUPIED EUROPE

KEY

- Greater Germany
- Territories under German occupation
- Italy and its territories
- Powers co-operating with the Axis
- Neutral countries
- Concentration camps

ROUTE TAKEN

- - -

Vienna
Cologne
Aachen (*now Aix-La-Chapelle*)
Verviers
Brussels
Antwerp
Merksplas
Eskaarde
Gent
Renaix
Tournai
Lille
St Cyprien
Gaillac
Brussels
Eskaarde
Paris
Figeac
Drancy
Auschwitz
Gleiwitz
Mittelbau-Dora via Vienna
Bergen-Belsen
Paris
USA

IRELAND

North Sea

UNITED KINGDOM

London

English Channel

to USA

The Hague
Antwerp
Eskaarde
Gent
Merksplas
Renaix
Brussels
Tournai
Lille
Aa
Verviers

NE

Paris
Drancy
BELGIUM

FRANCE

Bay of Biscay

Vichy

VICHY FRANCE

Figeac

Gaillac

St Cyprien

Bern
SW

Madrid

SPAIN

PORTUGAL

Mediterranean Sea

MOROCCO

ALGERIA

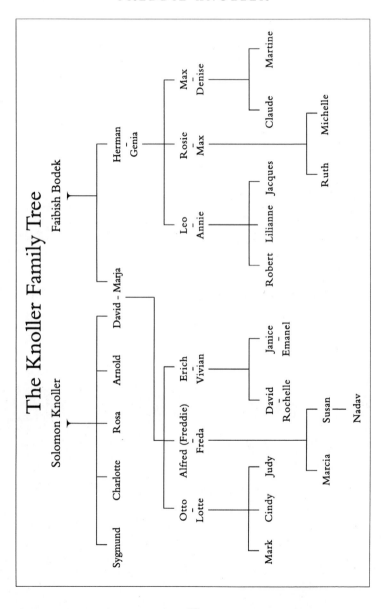

The Knoller Family Tree

Foreword

I FIRST met Freddie Knoller on a summer holiday in the 1980s, in the South of France. I already knew that he had been in the French Resistance and was a survivor of Auschwitz. When I asked him about his war he responded diffidently and I did not press him.

It was many years later that I sat next to Freddie at a family celebration. 'I am writing my memoirs, about my experiences and I have a manuscript, you know, but I cannot write well. I really need someone to help me.' I offered my services without hesitation, instinctively aware that I and Freddie – who accepted my offer at once – might be in for a long haul. It has taken six years to write this book.

Why? Putting aside all practical matters of mutual availability, with both Freddie and I working full time at the start of the project, it was in the nature of the manuscript that the real difficulties lay. On the one hand it was exiguous in the extreme, but on the other it contained an extraordinary story of risky flight, enemy interrogation, dangerous romance, escapes managed through sheer luck or boldness, and the sheer bloody-minded determination to survive three concentration camps and the notorious 'death marches'. But Freddie had somehow managed to give his extraordinary story the mundane quality of a shopping list. It was just a list of facts, a recounting of events that might have happened to some other person, a person of no particular consequence to Freddie Knoller.

When I tried to analyse what was awry with the narrative, I found it was, ironically, the absence of certain facts that deadened the material. And nearly all these 'facts' were associated with very important figures in the story. In the original manuscript I learnt nothing about how Freddie left the Hubermans, whose guest he was in Paris. One minute he was living with Otto in a small apartment, and the next he was working the red-light district with Christos. The filling in of this gap in the narrative was a major turning point in our work together: it uncovered the guilt Freddie has always felt at abandoning the 'Jewish-looking' Otto and escaping into the gentile world.

Then there was the matter of the gold coin, 'to be used in an emergency', that Freddie's mother sewed into his clothes when he was being prepared to leave Vienna. What happened to it? The text made no mention of it. Again, it was not that Freddie had forgotten – only that shame at his adolescent betrayal of a mother's loving thought prevented him from mentioning that he had to use it to pay his gambling debts in Belgium. Such examples could be multiplied many, many times, but, with their addition, the narrative became involving and much more substantial.

The survivors of Bergen-Belsen have been described by their deliverers as 'stony'. The trauma of their existences had left them almost without emotion. To survive it had been necessary to cauterise feeling. It proved hard to recover it. And this 'stoniness' characterised the original narrative.

Although these events have been recounted some sixty years after they occurred, memory was not so serious a problem as the above blockage. The starvation endured in the camps over a long

14

period does, it is well known, affect the memory. This is a result both of psychological trauma and the biological shrinkage of the cerebral cortex brought about by malnutrition. Freddie believed that he left Vienna with his cousin Maxl, but Maxl, who is alive and did not endure the camps, can confirm that this was not the case. He, with his family, had left that city of rampant antisemitism before Freddie did. Freddie does not remember Maxl being at Eksaarde with him, but he was. So there is a witness to certain events. Also, Freddie did start to recall details, no doubt as a result of both being immersed in the writing of the book and dealing with my questions. He remembered the appearance of the Hitler Youth at Auschwitz, and the song he sung to the Hungarian inmate towards the end of his time there.

As we drew near the end of the book I tried a new technique of extracting information from Freddie. As strange as it may sound, because I had a text before me, we had worked by my simply asking Freddie questions and he answering them – normally by email. In other words, a back-and-forth process – very exhausting – of amplifying and clarifying the material. But towards the end of the writing, as a result of a friend's suggestion, I began to interview Freddie with a tape recorder. The effect was immediate. Not only was I able better to pick up Freddie's way of expressing himself, which helped me greatly with dialogue, but it also enabled him simply to talk at will to a machine – a sort of third person in the room, a silent witness to his narrative – rather than the all-too-present me, haranguing poor him for more detail.

Working with Freddie has been exhilarating, infuriating, exhausting and uplifting by turns. Had I known how long the task was going to take, I still would have undertaken it. It has been, above all, a great privilege.

John Landaw

15

Introduction

IN MAY 1996 I travelled to Florida from my home in London for the funeral of my brother, Eric.

Some months after I returned to England a bulky parcel arrived from Eric's widow, Vivian. I opened it in a state of puzzlement and my eyes fell on a vast pile of correspondence. My heart suddenly racing, I saw the unmistakable elegant copperplate hand of my father. In her note, Vivian explained that she had come across this correspondence while sorting through Eric's personal effects and felt that I should have it, but hoped that I might translate it for her. She concluded by expressing her surprise at the existence of the letters, as Eric had never spoken of them.

At the foot of many of my father's letters were postscripts in my mother's hand and a few letters from my surviving brother, Otto. At a later date Vivian told me that she had sent another bundle of letters to him, but that he had found them too painful to read. I approached Otto, and he was only too pleased to send his bundle to me, so that I now possess the entire collection.

It was not difficult for me to understand Eric's silence over these letters. Following the Kristallnacht, Eric had been the son chosen to leave for America. This was because my parents laboured under

17

the naïve belief that his age made him the most vulnerable for military call-up. I entered Belgium illegally while Otto, after many difficulties, managed to reach England. It was to Eric, entirely safe in America, that my parents constantly wrote, begging him to do all in his power to facilitate their own emigration there. Every day since the fate of our parents became known to us after the war, Eric must have reproached himself for their murder. He had done all in his power to help them, but survivor guilt is not rational.

I, too, remained silent about my experiences until I was fifty-three, nearly thirty years after my liberation from Bergen-Belsen. Both my own survivor guilt and a desire to seal off my traumatic past, to try to begin life all over again, played their part. I did not remove the tattooed number, 157103, from my forearm, but neither did I display it. In keeping my parents' letters to him, perhaps Eric's behaviour was marked by the same ambivalence. My tattoo, a small piece of my concentration camp stripes and a red triangle which belonged to a dead French political prisoner, are the only physical relics of my war.

Then, during one traditional Friday-night family dinner, my eldest daughter, Marcia, who was then twenty, asked me to tell her about 'my life before'. Susie, my seventeen-year-old, quickly joined in: yes, it was now time to say something. What would she be able to tell her children about their grandfather's life? It was those words which made me respond. I thought, what do I know about my own parents' life before I was born? It is almost a blank. I was overcome with a powerful sense of something that might be lost for ever if I did not at last speak. I began my story and it was the early hours of the morning before I had finished it.

From that time on my recurring nightmares of endless flight and pursuit began to recede, but my former silent self has now been exchanged for a self who can never be silent.

I spend my waking hours involved in every aspect of Holocaust activities. It has become a mission, all-consuming, obsessive. I lecture, attend symposiums, give interviews, I attend a survivor's centre. And even when I am quiet, my story is replayed on monitors in the Holocaust Exhibition at the Imperial War Museum in London. And now, although I have written my book, I can see no end in sight to my need to communicate the experience of those years.

This book is not only meant as a legacy to posterity but as a personal memorial to my parents, whose graves I can never visit. Discovering their letters was the impetus which drove me to write it. I dedicate it to their lasting memory.

1

THE ISLAND OF MATZOS

SUNDAY 17 APRIL 1921, the day of my birth, was the first lovely day of spring, or so my mother always liked to tell me. I inherited my optimistic nature from my father, but it is also pleasant to believe that some guardian power granted sun on the day I entered the world. Because of one thing I am certain: it was only my optimistic nature and pure good luck that pulled me through the Nazi years.

I was the youngest of three sons and, although I was named Alfred, for as long as I can remember I have been called Freddie or Fredl. During my refugee years in Belgium I reverted to my original name. My *nom de guerre* in France was Robert. Later, in Auschwitz, my name was of no importance. I was simply 157103.

My parents, Marja and David, were born in Galicia, then part of Austria-Hungary. My mother came from Lemberg (Lvov) and my father from Dynov, both part of what became Poland once more at the end of the First World War. I believe that my grandfather, Schlomo, had moved to Vienna with my grandmother, Sara, to take a job in a bank but had then returned to Dynov, where my father was born in 1882. I am uncertain about these events because my parents spoke little of their life in Poland. It was as if they had disowned it, probably because being an *Ostjud* – a Jew from the East – was a stigma among Jews as well as gentiles.

I know that Father was in the Austrian Army in the First World War because he once showed us a photograph of himself in a uniform on a horse. At the side of the picture there was an anonymous hand holding the horse, which perhaps gave the game away because father had told us that he was a bookkeeper in the army. Perhaps the hand was a steadying one and Father's proud posture on the horse was just for the camera. He still possessed the sabre he wore in this picture, and kept it in our bedroom, wrapped in a soft cloth and out of our reach on the top of the wardrobe. Once in a while he would take down the sabre and polish it.

Ours was a typically lower middle-class Jewish family. My father was a bookkeeper for the Viennese wholesale fashion firm of Grossner & Weiss. It is the only job I remember him having, and he was openly very proud that he had worked for the same firm for so many years, but his pride in this achievement was a mask for his innate caution and lack of ambition. The owner of the company, Mr Herr, lived with his family in a luxurious villa on the outskirts of Vienna. He must have thought highly of my father because he once asked him to become a partner, but Father turned his boss down. 'Let him have the headaches,' he said to Mother. 'I'll have my wages.'

We lived in the second district of Vienna, Leopoldstadt, or, as the city's gentiles called it, Matzes Insel, the Island of Matzos.

22

Here we Jews were the majority and this made us feel secure. It was possible to forget that to be a Jew was to be a member of a small minority in Austria. In a way, one half of the antisemitic nickname for our neighbourhood was true, for we were insular and, in being insular, quite blind to the signs of the catastrophe which was to overtake us.

Our home was a two-roomed apartment at 32 Untere Augartenstrasse, a broad street with a busy tramway. We lived on the third floor, overlooking the inner courtyard. There was no lift in the building, for at that time these were found only in the most luxurious apartments.

Six of us, including the maid – not an unusual number in the Vienna of my youth – lived in two rooms. The apartment was typical of its kind. You entered through a heavy oak door and walked down a long passage. To the left was our kitchen, separated from the passage by a frosted-glass partition. Our maid slept in the kitchen on a camp bed. The living space was dominated by lumbering items of dark furniture; in the middle stood a heavy dining table surrounded by eight chairs, though this was extendable and could accommodate twelve people. Between two long windows covered by embroidered lace curtains was a tall grandfather clock, jealously guarded by my father. 'This is my clock,' he said. 'Only I touch it.' I liked to watch him remove the large key from the small shelf inside the great clock, too high for me to reach when I was young, and I would stand by fascinated as he inserted the key into the mechanism that cricked noisily as he turned. Sometimes he would adjust the clock by screwing the pan-shaped brass pendulum up or down the long threaded rod bisecting it. When Father was not in, I could not resist opening the glass panel at the front and touching this pendulum or marvelling

23

at the heaviness of the bomb-shaped weights as I held my hands under them.

In front of the clock stood brother Otto's Bosendorfer grand piano, my mother's pride and joy. The other conspicuous object in this room was a tiled oven, reaching almost to the ceiling. In winter a bucket full of coal and wood stood by it. Otto, my eldest brother, slept in this room on a large cream sofa next to Father's bookcase.

Father's bookcase was full of books about the First World War. I loved the photographs of tanks and artillery, even of poor dead or wounded soldiers. Weighty encyclopedias often provided answers for my homework. There was a large art book. The painters may have been famous but it was their depictions of nude women which interested me.

By my bed in one corner was another tiled oven similar to the one in the living room. In the only other room slept the remainder of the family. All our family's clothes were contained in two very large wardrobes that had doors of a highly polished, light coloured wood. It still amazes me how we managed to live so on top of one another, but we did.

We had no bathroom, so after school on Fridays we went to the nearby Diana Bad, a public bathing house ten minutes' walk away, near the Augarten Brücke, a bridge over the Danube Canal. In the corridor was a basin, with cold running water only, which we shared with the tenants of the two adjoining apartments. There was no heating out there, and no light in the toilet, which was in a separate room opposite the basin. Each of the apartments had a key for the toilet; ours hung in the kitchen, and I would sit in the toilet by the dim light of a candle and devour the books forbidden by my father. Soon enough I would be sighing in

24

frustration as I heard the sound of another key fiddling at the lock. The books I would read in secret were cheap paperbacks containing mildly adult material. I remember to this day the hero of most of these books: Tom Shark, a detective. Father destroyed one once, which was why I took to reading in the toilet. I also loved the Wild West adventure stories of Karl May, a popular young person's author. Father approved of those.

My parents were acquaintances of the Aments, who lived in our apartment block. Sometimes they would meet at the Augarten Kaffeehaus, near the Augarten Brücke. People of our social class rarely entertained at home, our apartments being so small, so the coffee house was our meeting place. The Aments were a very good-looking family, the boys tall and fair. Their daughter, Fritzi, was beautiful even as a child, with blonde hair and a button nose. One day when we both twelve years old we locked ourselves in the toilet. We stood in front of each other. It was an I'll-show-you-mine-if-you show-me-yours encounter. It was quickly over because Fritzi was terrified of discovery, and afterwards we never spoke of the incident.

At home we spoke German, never Yiddish, and apart from the odd Yiddish word in common usage, I do not know if my parents even knew the language. Perhaps it was through the same fear of being labelled *Ostjuden* that they did not speak Yiddish. My father's perfect German suggested that he was educated in a German school, but I'm not sure about this. If our parents did not want us to understand them, it was Polish they spoke. I tried to speak German as well as my father but, in the company of school friends, Viennese slang naturally crept in.

Father's handwriting was exemplary. Elegant, regular and easy to understand, it was no more than an extension of his

25

personality: clear and to the point. We always knew where we were with Father. Mother was untidy and warm-hearted and always jumping from one subject to the next, confident that you were having no difficulty in following her train of thought. Her handwriting was as wayward and as indecipherable as she was. For her the heart was everything; nothing else mattered.

Vienna was everything to us, our whole world – almost a city of Jews, we sometimes proudly felt – for were not the names of many of its most famous sons Jewish? In the theatre the works of Arthur Schnitzler were produced more than those of any other playwright. The producer Max Reinhardt had founded the Salzburg Festival. Vienna was the birthplace and home of Arnold Schoenberg, who succeeded Gustav Mahler, another Jew who had made this most musical city his home. In the genre of Viennese operetta the half-Jewish Johann Strauss family had been succeeded by Emmerich Kalman and Oscar Strauss. In cabaret Fritz Grünbaum and Karl Farkas were very popular, as were the comedians Hermann Leopoldi, Franz Engel and Armin Berg. Of the four Austrian Nobel prizes for medicine, three went to Jews – Karl Landsteiner for discovering and classifying the blood types, Otto Loewy for his discoveries in muscle chemistry, and Baron Clemens Pirquet, who devised the test for tuberculosis. And of course, with Freud, psychoanalysis was born in Vienna.

The influence and achievement of Jews in Viennese society gave us a sense of belonging which was to prove entirely delusory, for the reality of our daily lives was that we mixed socially only with Jews, merely exchanging greetings with our Christian neighbours. Though there was nothing in appearance to distinguish us from each other, we remained strangers. But I had only to walk around the corner into Schrey Gasse or Malz Gasse to be in a world which was as alien to me as to the Christians: the closed living places of the ultra-orthodox, through which my family passed only *en route* to somewhere else. Heavily bearded men in black carrying prayer books under their arms, their features indistinct under black hats, moved along the streets in groups. Young boys, also dressed in black, played in the streets, their heads covered with small skullcaps, their long earlocks flying about as they chased a ball. The women shopped and clustered together in conversation, their colourful headscarves inb sharp contrast to the sombre attire of the men. As dusk fell on Friday the shops closed and the streets became quiet. Now the men wore the *Shtramel*, the wide, fur-brimmed hat originally worn by the Polish nobility, as they honoured the Sabbath (in their own *Shul*, or synagogue). To them we were scarcely Jews at all. Our Polnische Tempel was as foreign to them as a Christian church.

Musicians regularly came into our courtyard to play sentimental Jewish Melodies; sometimes we heard the plangent sounds of accordions and trumpets or the plaintive voice of a singer. Mother always taught us to be charitable to the poor. 'They have little,' she would say, 'perhaps no work, and a hungry family to support.' She would give me a few coins, which I would wrap in paper and throw down to the players. There was a particular couple that stood out for me – she on the violin and he the guitar – who, in my memory, always seemed to receive the most money from the residents.

That the Knoller boys played musical instruments was typically Viennese. It was our parents' delight to hear us play; six was the age at which each of us was introduced to a musical instrument. Mother and Father already had a duet, Otto playing piano and Eric violin. (Eric was originally Erich, of course, but, as things

27

turned out, I knew him for most of his life by the English form of the name.) With the arrival of my sixth birthday the choice of the cello for me was inevitable. Now my parents would at last have their trio.

My first teacher came weekly to our apartment and taught me for one hour. Mother ensured that I practised for half an hour every day, checking the time by her watch, but I took to the instrument, so that playing was not a hardship for me. I used to love the deep, sonorous gong of the grandfather clock as it marked the hour and when I practised I would interrupt my scales or pieces to imitate its tone with a deep note on my cello.

I must have reached a decent standard because four years later my teacher suggested I take an examination for the Music Academy of Vienna. I passed quite easily and started classes under Professor Buxbaum, who played with the famous Rosé Quartet. At first my mother accompanied me on the half-hour tram ride to the imposing Academy, situated near the Stadtpark, but she quickly trusted me to make my own way there.

I enjoyed lessons at the Academy. There were five other young cellists, and the Professor – a Jew, I believe, an imposingly tall, handsome man – set each of us the task of playing sections of a sonata and then invited us to comment critically on the performance we had just heard. The following player had to improve on what we had just heard, and we were sent away with instructions on what and how to practise. In winter I used to linger outside before catching the tram, because there was a large skating rink there. I loved to stand and watch the experts glide over the ice and the beginners slip on it.

When I was twelve the professor began teaching me privately at his home. Whether there was any significance in this venue I

do not know, but my mother believed he only taught
I possessed an exceptional talent.

Mother was actively involved in the Jewish charity Wizo, the
Women's International Zionist Organisation, and the Knoller
boys played at such events. The programme would often contain
a well-known and well-worn medley of Jewish music called *Altes
aus dem Osten* (Old Tunes from the East). The arranger of these
medleys was Isy Geiger, who later emigrated to England and
became a quite well-known band leader. I still have a programme
for the occasion when we played Haydn's Trio No. 1 in G, on 9
April 1932 – I was almost eleven – at a parents' concert at our
school, the Sperl Gymnasium. Mother had tears of pride in her
eyes that day. Soon afterwards we started performing regularly at
concerts arranged by Otto's teacher, Millie Kozack.

Father had his seat at the local synagogue, the striking, domed
Polnische Tempel. He was an attender only on high days and holy
days, not being a very religious man.

On Friday nights, after the traditional candlelit Sabbath meal, we
played at home. A religious widow called Mrs Kohn sometimes
joined us for dinner, insisting on bringing her own kosher food
with her, and I remember how delicious her boiled chicken was,
particularly with the dill she added, not a herb my mother used in
this way. She would have been horrified to discover that ham was
a special treat Mother served us when we were ill. After the meal
we all sang the latest popular songs from sheet music which Otto
obtained from the music publishers Francis Day, and then we boys
went eagerly to our instruments and played light chamber music
and popular arrangements. Gershwin and Rodgers and
Hammerstein were particular favourites.

I was a skinny, frail little boy, short-sighted from the age of six,

29

and watched over anxiously by my mother. The local doctor, Dr Friedmann, knew me well, because I caught colds easily and marked every icy Vienna winter with a bout of tonsillitis. Mother made me gargle disgusting medicine. I was quite immature compared with my brothers – a real mother's boy. I inherited my friendly nature from her. In any crowd of strangers I need to make a contact, with a word, a smile, or simply a nod. Though Otto is similar to me in this way, this trait is stronger in me, perhaps the need of a survivor of the camps to ensure that the stranger is not an enemy.

I was six years old when I entered the *Volksschule*, or elementary school, in Leopoldgasse, not far from my home, and it was here that I first experienced antisemitism. *'Sau Jud!* Jew pig!' called other six-year-olds after us, and spat at us. I decided that the next time this happened I would fight my tormentor. Soon enough the familiar taunt was hurled in my direction and I turned and punched the boy on the nose. Blood streamed from his face and his friends set upon me, beating me with their heavy satchels. I ran home, clothes torn and body bruised. 'How did you get in this state?' asked my mother anxiously, and I told her. Her response deflated all my pride in my fighting spirit. 'You must not get into fights, especially with Christian children. If they insult you, just ignore it.' Father, returning home later from business, supported my mother entirely.

I was utterly bewildered by their attitude, too young to understand their ancient Jewish fear of rousing gentile wrath and reprisal. Yet the very next day the boy whose nose I had bloodied wanted to make friends with me.

'Look,' he said gruffly, 'that was not a fair fight. Five on to one is not fair.'

'Thanks,' I said, glad of his support. He had a boy's approach to these matters of honour, far removed from my parents' incomprehensible pacifism. 'I'm Karl Swoboda,' he said.

We started talking and quickly discovered our shared enthusiasm for stamp collecting. Karl was a typical Austrian Christian, fair-haired and blue-eyed and always wearing the traditional Austrian dress of lederhosen, green jacket and white knee socks. Sometimes he also wore the hat with a feather in the crown. Sometimes I went to his home, in a poor neighbourhood near ours, where his mother was always kind to me. Yet my parents forbade me to bring any Christian boy into the apartment. I remember once asking Karl about his ancestry. With a name like Swoboda he must have had Czech ancestors, I suggested. 'Never!' he said, 'I am Austrian, pure Austrian!' I was astonished by the vehemence of his denial.

Karl did not follow me into the Gymnasium. He was not a bright boy and so must have failed, or not even taken, the entrance examination and gone on to an ordinary secondary school. We still met sometimes, but it was only our passion for stamps which now connected us.

I was friendly with only one other gentile. This was Mr Hagmann, the caretaker of our apartment block, who lived with his wife and son in our building. He was a tall, well-built man, whose receding hair made him look old – I seem to remember that he was only in his forties. He was a polite and gentle person, much liked by the tenants. He was also an avid philatelist and we often pored over his beautifully kept collection of Austrian stamps and exchanged items. Sometimes Karl joined us. I never sensed any antisemitism in Mr Hagmann, who was proud of being a socialist.

At the Gymnasium, where seventy per cent or so of the pupils were Jewish, I was as proud of our Austrian history as any other student. Was not my very own district named after Kaiser Leopold? That king's expulsion of Austrian Jews and the anti-Jewish sentiments of another Austrian idol, Maria Theresa, were as unknown to me as the pogroms against the Jews by the crusaders under the leadership of Richard the Lionheart, a man I admired for his heroism in conquering the Holy Land.

Jews received separate religious instruction. This might now seem, in a multicultural society, an enlightened state of affairs, but in Vienna it only seemed to accentuate our difference from our gentile school fellows.

Our religious teacher, Professor Glaser, was the archetype of the soft, ineffectual Jew. We did not show him the respect due to a teacher and thought him a real *nebbich* – a hopeless person inspiring pity. We ran rings round the poor old gentleman, with his wispy white beard and thick-framed glasses from behind which his magnified eyes darted helplessly about as we talked through the entire lesson.

I was ten years old when I was allowed to join the boy scouts. How I loved the uniform, with the wide-brimmed Mafeking hat! And giving the scout salute, raising three fingers to the brim of the hat and exclaiming, *'All Zeit Bereit!* Be prepared!'

The scout movement lived up to its internationalist ideals: I never found antisemitism here. Only the pleasure of roaming the Wiener Wald, the Vienna Woods, with my fellow scouts, imagining ourselves to be the intrepid heroes of our adventure books, or sitting around the campfire, singing and listening to stories told by the scoutmaster. I made a friend there, another Jewish boy, from my own school, called Hans Schwarz. I called him Hansl and he remained a friend for many years. He lived near me in Rembrandt

Strasse, where I visited him often. His apartment was similar to mine, except that his mother was rarely there, so I assume that she must have worked, which was unusual for a woman of her background. He had some fascinating toys, whereas I had very few of my own. Some of his were very sophisticated, needing batteries. All I had at home was a type of Lego set, known as a Matador, with which I was not especially adept. The marvellous possibilities of these building bricks was quite beyond me, but Hansl was a master of his, creating all kinds of complicated structures, and I envied him this gift with his hands.

It was Hansl who, about two years later, introduced me to another social organisation: the Kinderfreunde. Father approved whole-heartedly of my membership of this club because, like so many social organisations in Vienna, this one also had a political affiliation, to Father's Social Democrat Party. Many of the members were Jewish. Father was also aware that the organiser of the club was an ex-teacher, who insisted that we did our homework before engaging in the club activities. The organiser subjected us to serious lectures, comparing dictatorships, such as Hitler's Germany or Italy's Mussolini, with good democracies. He urged us to be proud of our 'working-class roots'. But I enjoyed the greeting of 'Freundschaft! Friendship!' we gave each other, which made me feel part of a select, powerful and grown-up group. We sang a special song at the beginning of each meeting: '*Wir sind jung, die Welt ist offen!* We are young and the world awaits us!'

At the age of thirteen I went through the traditional barmitzvah ceremony, at the Polnische Tempel. Afterwards we all gathered in our apartment for a festive meal. Barmitzvah celebrations then were not the grand affairs they often are now,

33

so there were only thirteen of us there. There was Uncle Hermann, my mother's brother, his wife Genya and their children, Rosi, Leo and Maxl. They lived in the Simmering district, on the outskirts of Vienna – a poor neighbourhood. Naturally our neighbours Mrs Kohn, Miss Schiff and her brother – a ministry official who was always addressed by his title of Herr Regierungsrat – were also guests. None of Father's family were present, as none of them lived in Austria. I remember a gift of a book from my brothers – the latest Karl May adventure; from Miss Schiff a beautiful wooden chess set, whose box was inlaid with the board; and from my parents the most treasured gift: a wristwatch with a brown leather strap – a really grown-up present. Father insisted I wear it only on special occasions, and never at school. For my barmitzvah my brothers and I had rehearsed some pieces: Grieg's *Norwegian Dances*, along with the latest music from the American musical cinema, mainly Fred Astaire numbers, I remember.

That barmitzvah celebration was in early 1934. Who among that group could have known that, in a mere four years, Austria would be a dangerous country for them to live in?

My father was a heavily built man with a chubby face, and very much taller than my mother. I remember him having a moustache when I was very young, but this he later shaved off. He said he removed it because he wanted to look young, but perhaps it was because he was aware of the contrast with his bald head. Wherever Father went he always wore a tie. I cannot remember ever seeing him in casual clothes. His expression was genuinely kindly – he would show his love for his children, perhaps when we had achieved something scholastically or on relaxed family outings to the Vienna Woods, when we sang

34

together. But he could be very stern if we earned his disapproval and would not hesitate to deprive us of pocket money or smack us. Afterwards it was Mother who comforted us. Father's code was a simple and unbending one, right and wrong clear and unambiguous concepts for him. A good slap and they won't do it again, was his belief. He kept a cane for serious offences.

I remember the day when Hansl and I decided to climb the wooden structure of the swimming-pool entrance at the Kay Park. We had almost reached the roof when my father's voice reached my ears. 'Come down immediately!' he called up sharply. Father was on his way home, and his route took him through the park, which was fifteen minutes from our home. Father and I walked home in silence and I knew I was in for a beating. 'Go and wait in the bedroom!' he ordered when we arrived.

I had a little time and I grabbed one of the small cushions which lay on top of the bed and stuffed it down my trousers. Father came into the bedroom with a carpet-beater and told me to bend over the bed. After two whacks, he felt at my bottom. He burst out laughing and took me in his arms. 'You're a clever boy, but promise me you will never play such dangerous games again.' I promised and, still laughing, he kissed me. That was my father, quick to anger and quick to forget.

Education was very important to him, especially in a society where Jews were excluded from a number of professions. Ever anxious to foster an enquiring mind in his sons, he was at pains to answer all our questions and I remember what a good listener he was, seeming to take in every word we said with an acute expression on his face. There was little room to make a fool of yourself when someone was listening like that. With such a cast of mind it was hard for Father to accept that Eric, often found asleep over his books, was no academic. One day Eric came home with a bad school report. Father chased him round the table, nearly tripping over one of the legs in his angry pursuit.

Finally Father got the message and sent Eric to work in Grossner & Weiss, where he himself was employed. Eric was only a messenger boy and cleaner there, but he greatly preferred this to school.

Even so, Father and Eric still clashed a great deal. Father was a socialist, but Eric joined a militant right-wing Zionist organisation called Betar, which Father could not abide. 'I do not want a son of mine doing military drill!' he bellowed.

'How are we going to fight the Arabs and the British to make a homeland for the Jews if we don't train like soldiers?' Eric argued back, and remained in Betar, perhaps to establish his independence from our controlling father.

Father clashed less often with Otto. I remember only one particular incident. Otto had become very fond of a girl called Lotte (though none of us was allowed to bring girls into the apartment). One day Father forbade Otto ever to see Lotte again. The reason? He had discovered that her sister was a divorced woman.

This father, so strict with us, was nevertheless putty in Mama's hands. He could refuse her nothing. It was only in the outer world, the world of men and their transactions, that she relied entirely on his judgement and this was, in the end, a tragedy for both of them. For Father's belief in the simple and predictable, and above all the essential decency of people, meant that he could not begin to envisage the nature of the disaster soon to engulf us all.

If I wanted something, it was to my mother I went. Mama could persuade Father about almost anything to do with her sons. She was quite short, rather plump but with a kind, round face framed appealingly by soft, fair hair. Conscious of her figure, she always wore a *Mieder*, a kind of corset, when she went out, to make her look slimmer. Mother was carefree and warm in spirit, whereas Father, despite his optimistic nature, was a stiff person. She loved people and she adored dancing. My young cousin Rosi was very happy to have her socially adept and easy-going aunt as her chaperone at Jewish charity tea dances.

During the day we would hear Mama's soft, absent whistling around the house. We children lived in her heart and she did not disguise this fact. Tears of pride were never far from her eyes as the audience clapped the Knoller brothers performing their medley of music on stage at Wizo fund-raising events. It was a classic attraction of opposites between her and Father.

It was in 1934, the year of my barmitzvah, that I joined the Realgymnasium in Sperlgasse. In charge of physical training was Professor Meyer. He was bald, short and broad-shouldered, his arms bulging with muscles. He had a hard stare and loved to ridicule Jews who were less athletic than the rest of the class. 'Come on,' he'd say, 'you're not in the synagogue now.'

As I grew older, so my life split between my Jewishness and my socialism. This split was also in evidence among my friends. We would meet outside the synagogue on Saturday mornings, paying a sort of guilty lip service to the fact that we were Jews and this was the Sabbath, but then we did not go in, but went off to talk about socialism, Zionism and girls.

At the age of fifteen I joined the Verein der Sozialistischen Mittelschüler, the Association of Socialist High School Students. It was natural to do so. The Jews voted Social Democrat because the left was not rooted in antisemitism, standing as it did for values other than race and nation. This was demonstrated by the fact that Jews, such as Victor Adler, Otto Bauer and Julius Tandler, held prominent positions in the party. Vienna was run by the Social Democrats, while the nation was in the hands of the conservative Christian Social Party. Though retaining its clerical antipathy to Jews, the party had no sympathy for the National Socialist Party, who were anti-Catholic. The Nazis, who were in a minority, were a nuisance, but their importance, it was generally felt, was not to be exaggerated.

On 12 February 1934 the lights in our classroom suddenly went out. The headmaster appeared. 'A general strike has been declared by the unions. You are all to go home.' Of course, the trade unions were part of my Social Democrat party, but this was a matter of indifference to me, to Hansl or to any other of our classmates. We were all merely delighted with this unexpected holiday. Rushing gleefully out of school, we were surprised into silence by the stillness of the streets. Nobody was about. The trams were stationary. Vienna seemed to be a city abandoned. I made my way home through empty streets, to find the whole family at home and candles giving the only light in the apartment.

We heard the sound of gunfire. Father spoke gravely. 'I saw the Heimwehr and police everywhere. I can only think they are fighting the Social Democrats over at the Gemeinde Häuser.' Later came the boom of artillery. Mother was upset but the sound thrilled me, and my brothers looked equally stirred. At one point Father turned on the radio, but it was dead. The next morning the power came back on, and from the radio we understood that the Army had indeed fired on the Gemeinde Häuser, the large apartment blocks built by the Socialists for the workers, which had been occupied during the trouble by the socialist Schutzbund. The Heimwehr had been refused entry and fired upon. Many innocent people died in their homes, yet I have to say that I enjoyed the atmosphere of all this instability and confrontation.

After a few days normality returned to our lives, but the political situation in Austria continued to be volatile. Violence had become the political language of Austria. Each political faction had its militant wing – the Nazis the Brownshirts, the Christian Socialists the Heimwehr and the Democrats the Schutzbund. Although Chancellor Dollfuss had banned the Nazi Party, they continued to agitate. Perhaps because we thought of the Nazis as a lunatic fringe, my father and Otto thought that the danger to the Jews came more from the tiny Chancellor Dollfuss and his Christian Socialist Party than from the Nazis, because the popular Christian Socialists retained their antipathy to Jews. Dollfuss – known as Millimetternich because of his diminutive height and his desire to emulate the great Metternich – had the courage to outlaw the Nazis, but was then assassinated by them on 25 July during an abortive putsch.

Otto came home from the University with reports of Nazi students beating Jewish students. 'In a few days there is going to be a big protest about this,' he announced. My own Association of Socialist High School Students was invited to join the demonstration. Full of excitement, I went along with Hansl and another close friend of mine, Freddie Breitfeld. The protest was held in the great hall on Schwarzenburg Platz. Armed police separated the socialists from the Nazis. The Nazis were seated in the balcony and they disrupted the speeches, shouting their slogan down at the socialists in the body of the hall: *'Deutschland Erwache! Juda Verrecke!* Germany, awake! Let the Jews perish!' They catcalled and sang the *Horst Wessel Lied*, which tells of the joy of Jewish blood dripping from Nazi knives. I knew this song well and loved its fierce, marching rhythm. The horrible words excited me and made me long for a fight.

After the assassination of Dollfuss, which did not alert my father or most other Jews to the truth of the situation in Austria, my father welcomed Chancellor Schuschnigg, whom he considered a moderate, but the treaty signed between Germany and Austria 'normalising' relations worried our family. We had heard the reports of Hitler's treatment of the Jews. 'Jews are leaving Germany. What does this treaty with Germany mean to us here?' asked Father, 'we know what Hitler does with treaties.' Nobody really seemed to know which way the wind was blowing. The Nazis were still banned, but German newspapers, available again in Austria after this treaty, painted a rosy picture of Hitler's Germany.

In 1935 I fell in love for the first time. We were spending a summer at Lake Balaton, in Hungary, and that holiday place will always be associated in my mind with pretty, buxom Rosza, who looked older than her age, while I looked younger than mine. Rozsa turned my head and I thought she must be in love with me, but she was just testing her effect on the opposite sex, and I was as good a subject for her experiments as any other male. She was staying in the same hotel as my family, and I sought her out. I also knew that she walked along the promenade with her friends, as people did then, to see and be seen. One morning I saw her leaving the hotel with a group of friends. Knowing that I would be completely tongue-tied if I engineered crossing her path, I quickly picked a single flower from the hotel garden. I caught up with her group and held it out to her. This was how I demonstrated I cared for her. She took my flower graciously, with a little giggle.

My brother Eric was sixteen, taller than me by several inches, and good-looking. A few days later I saw Rosza walking with him and I was gripped with jealousy, miserably understanding that I couldn't compete with my older brothers. It was bad enough to be excluded from their conversations about sex, but this defeat seemed altogether too much to bear. I cursed my baby face and the glasses stuck on it that made me look so studious. I was second best and that was it. I was far too young to see Eric's shyness and uncertainty, which originated, I am sure, in Father's disappointment at his academic weakness. Eric had already left school, Otto was studying medicine at the University, and I was in high school.

As for Otto, he was clever, but also a light-hearted fellow, popular with everybody, including girls. Of course, I wanted to be around my brothers, copying what I saw as their grown-up ways. But I was a kid to them, jovially patronised and never included in their private affairs, despite the fact that Eric was much nearer in age to me – two years older – than he was to Otto, who was six years older than him. I was just their baby brother, perhaps also because Mama treated me like one.

At home it was the same story. In her apartment across the courtyard, Miss Pollack had the habit of undressing in front of her window. Otto and Eric whispered together as they studied her through binoculars. By the time my Peeping Tom brothers handed the binoculars over to me, Miss Pollack had her nightdress on, and this seemed to confirm that all three of them were engaged in some unspoken conspiracy against me: such sights, they all understood, were not for the eyes of the young.

But I was obsessed with thoughts of sex. I wanted sex for itself, and to put myself on the same level as my brothers.

Theresa – Resi for short – was our maid. I was sixteen. It was

41

no sign of affluence in the Vienna of those days to have a maid. These girls came from poor peasant families, smallholders for whom making any sort of living was very hard and supporting growing offspring impossible. The girls came to the city to seek domestic employment. The wages were not high, but they learnt to cook and sew and care for a family and received free board and lodging.

One evening when my parents were out with friends and my brothers at the cinema, I lay in bed thinking about sex while Resi slept on her folding bed in the kitchen area. On the pretext of getting water from the kitchen, I ended up sitting on her bed. She didn't seem to mind when I began caressing her bosom. I got into bed with her, and she touched me where I had never been touched before. I couldn't control myself and in my naivety thought I was urinating, and was ashamed. She just giggled at the mess I made. I muttered an apology and left. A fiasco, but enough of an experience to share with Hansl and Freddie in the Kay Park the very next day. As we sat on a bench and talked, it was my puzzlement as much as the desire to boast that drove me. 'One thing I can't understand,' I began hesitantly. 'What?' urged my friends. 'Well, why was it that I started peeing when she touched my *Schmeckl*? But my nightshirt was sticky, not wet.' The pair of them burst out laughing. 'All right, what's so funny?' I was offended, and embarrassed as well, because they obviously knew something I didn't. 'You idiot,' cried Hansl between fits of laughter, 'that's what happens down there when you ejaculate. What comes out of your *Schmeckl*, well, that's the stuff that makes babies! You didn't know that?' More laughter from my friends. This was my first lesson in matters sexual.

The year 1938 started with a ferment of political activity. Every accessible surface of the city was covered with political posters and stickers urging people to vote one way or the other in the forthcoming referendum. Just as I collected stamps, so Eric collected these, peeling them from wall and lamppost and sticking them neatly in an album. What a historical document they would have made! But Father, in a rage with Eric over something or other, tore the collection to pieces in front of us – a quite uncharacteristic action for him – which shocked me deeply, as it seemed so wrong, so unfair. 'You have destroyed my labour of love!' Eric shouted at Father, and I could only stand by silently.

Because of events in Germany the Nazis were daily growing in confidence. They demonstrated and chanted with increasing vociferousness for *'Ein Volk, ein Reich, ein Führer'*. The Schutzbund responded with calls for Austria's independence. The ruling Christian Socialists under Schuschnigg were for Austria's continuing independence, but they were fearful of the big German nation. Austria was in turmoil. There were soon daily fights between Nazi and anti-Nazi students. Once Otto returned from the University with a bloody face. Under Austrian law the police had no jurisdiction to intervene because the clashes were on the University's premises. Until now only very few Jews really understood what particular beast was awakening. These few included my school friend Freddie Breitfeld's father, who had transferred his fur business to England as far back as 1936.

The referendum on the momentous issue of Austrian independence was set for 10 April 1938. It was fairly certain that the Christian Socialists would prevail. Late in the afternoon on that Thursday the whole family crowded anxiously round the radio. There had been a rumour for hours that the plebiscite was going to be cancelled. An ominously vague announcement that we were to stand by for an important statement lent credence to this rumour. At seven-thirty that evening Schuschnigg finally addressed the nation:

'Austrian men and women! This day has brought us face to face with a serious and decisive decision... The government of the German Reich has presented an ultimatum to the Federal President demanding that he appoint a candidate chosen by the Reich Government to the office of Chancellor... Should the Federal President not accept this ultimatum then German troops will cross our border this very hour... The Federal President has instructed me to inform the nation that we are giving way to brute force ... we refuse to shed German blood ... we have ordered our armed forces to withdraw without serious resistance... So in this hour I bid farewell to the people of Austria with a German word and a wish from the bottom of my heart: "God Save Austria."'

We listened in stunned disbelief, and then came the soft playing of the Austrian national anthem, Haydn's *Emperor Quartet*, the same as the German one, after which nothing came from the radio but the empty crackle of static. Father was pale, still looking at the radio, as if to will a revocation of the terrible statement we had just heard. At fifty-six he looked old, I suddenly noticed, ready for retirement, and now he had this to face. Mother cried and Father put his arm round her shoulder. Otto looked angry. The very next day was Eric's birthday, but no one was thinking of it.

That morning German troops entered Austria and the two countries became one. There was no such country as Austria any longer. The Anschluss had made us a province of Germany called Ostmark.

We decided to stock up with food, not knowing what the next few days would bring. I went with Mother to the shops. I think she wanted me, the youngest, at her side. On the staircase we encountered Herr Hagmann, now wearing a Nazi armband. This decent man greeted us with a guilty expression and a sheepish 'Good morning'.

There was a sad irony in this. Less than a year earlier I had gone down to knock on Herr Hagmann's door on the off chance that he might have some new stamps to show me. In 1934, following the assassination of Dollfuss, Chancellor Schuschnigg had banned all opposition parties. When Mr Hagmann had opened the door to me, he saw me gaze at once at the three-arrow badge on his lapel, the symbol of the Social Democrats, the party our family supported. He had invited me in but, clearly embarrassed, had removed his jacket. Now, for entirely opposite reasons, he found himself embarrassed before me again.

Out in the streets my mother and I saw swastika flags hanging from the windows of almost every home. Brown-shirted Nazis of the *Sturmabteilung*, or SA, roamed the streets. We saw them stopping conspicuously Jewish-looking men and forcing them to clean away the plebiscite slogans. Further along the street was a sight that chilled our blood. SA men continuously kicked an old bearded Jew in the backside as he tried to scrape a slogan from the pavement. All around gentile Austrians, some of them women with infants, laughed uproariously.

Severely shaken, we returned home as quickly as possible with our supplies. We had enough to withstand a siege, because the siege mentality had now entered us. My brothers and my father were still gathered around the radio, because there was no question of Father going to work or Otto to his classes. When we

45

recounted what we had witnessed on the streets Father told us of exultant reports proclaiming that the German troops had received a tremendous welcome from the Austrian populace. Although we knew that the radio was in the hands of the new regime, from what my mother and I had seen we had no reason to doubt the general truth of these reports. Father told us that the commentator had described a mass Austrian Nazi rally on the Ring Strasse. Arthur Seyss-Inquart, the new head of state, had spoken on the radio, telling us that the cause of all Austria's problems was the Jews, not only Austrian Jewry, but world Jewry, which controlled every country not only financially, but also morally. This was but one of a score of antisemitic speeches we heard that day. The Nazi slogan *'Die Juden sind unser Unglück.* The Jews are our misfortune,' rang out again and again, along with Deutschland über alles.

That evening Mother cried fitfully while the telephone rang non-stop. Everyone was calling everyone else not just to discuss the situation, but to seek the reassurance of friends' voices. But how blithely confident Father remained throughout it all! At some point the telephone rang for Otto. Afterwards he said, 'It was a friend. He wants to escape to Italy and he has asked me to join him, but it must be tonight.' Father dismissed this. 'Your friend is a *meshuggena*,' he said. 'Hitler will march in and he'll march out. Forget Italy.' And Otto did, which almost cost him his life. Despite Father's confidence, we spent the rest of the night listening anxiously to the radio, as if trying to set our compass by it. Our neighbour and close friend Miss Schiff came to us in tears. 'What shall we do? What shall we do?' she kept repeating, like a chant. My father tried to comfort her. 'Don't worry, they won't hurt us, we are the old ones. But the children, they have to leave, there is no future for them here.' Miss Schiff told us that she had a cousin in Miami. 'Maybe he can help,' she said. 'Mr Apte is a rich man, with an orange-canning factory. Then there is my other cousin in Antwerp, Jos Apte, a diamond merchant.' She promised to write to both her relatives and we thanked her with all our hearts.

One shopping trip with my mother I remember particularly well. I hated shopping and so would wait outside for her. I liked watching the people passing by and, yes, gazing at the dramatic red, black and white of the swastika flags hanging from almost every window. Then I saw a familiar figure approach. It was Karl Swoboda, smartly dressed in a Hitler Youth uniform, but the uniform did not deter me. I would speak to him. Hadn't we spent many hours together over our stamps, even if we were not close friends any more? As I opened my mouth to greet him I saw that Karl had seen me, but he looked straight ahead. I called after him, 'What's the matter? Don't you say hello?' He walked on, as determined to disown me as he had been his Czech ancestry, I suspected. Very upset, I told my mother about the incident. She hardly knew Karl, but dealt with the matter swiftly. 'He's had his mind turned by the Hitler Youth leaders. Perhaps this will teach you not to be friends with the goyim.'

So this meant we could be sure of no friend beyond another Jew. Yet, more than any of my mother's words, it was this personal incident with Karl that made me realise how much and how irredeemably things had changed for the Jews. And then, in the following days, came reports of the arrest of Jews and other dissident elements. The well-known luxury Metropole hotel had become the Gestapo's headquarters. From here Jews were deported to Dachau.

Hitler had moved only step by step against the Jews in

Germany, but by 1938 the quickening momentum of persecution hit the Austrian Jews all at once and so we had very little time to prepare for it. German Jews had at least had the benefit, if one might call it that, of six years of gradual erosion of their civil liberties to anticipate worse to follow.

Otto, Eric and I became part of the flood of people seeking to emigrate to any country that would take us. Our parents, hanging on to the belief that they were safe because of their age, thought only of America. All of us had registered at the US embassy, yet America was one of the most difficult countries for our parents to enter; the 'Polish Quota' was enormous, simply because so many Jews seeking escape, like my parents, had been born in Poland, and it was by country of birth that applicants were categorised. Although the embassy had assured our family that Otto, Eric and I, because we were born in Austria, would have no problem emigrating to America, we still had to wait. So we tried every other embassy we could think of, especially when there was a rumour that this or that country was issuing visas. But whenever we arrived there were always hundreds of others in front of us who had heard the same rumour. We tried the embassies of Chile, Peru, Ecuador, Uruguay... I got to know the names of virtually every South American country. Once we nearly managed to get a visa for Shanghai, which had its own independent consulate, but were sent home with only two people in front of us.

Jews were speedily banned from attending school with Christians. The only training permitted was in vocational institutions, so my parents entered me into the Tailoring Academy in Vienna. We had been used to restrictions in education and opportunities for Jews before Hitler. It had been almost impossible, for example, for a Jew to become an engineer

48

in Austria. Now came something else: we were to be all but returned to the ghetto.

Our dear neighbour Miss Schiff had been working very hard to ensure the safety of the Knoller boys and one day she came to us with the news that her Apte cousins in Florida could sponsor one of us. Mother and Father must have debated this quandary anxiously: to which of their boys to allot this haven of safety. In the end they decided to send Eric because, in their pathetic assumption that the Nazis would have some proper use for the Jews, they feared that he was the most eligible for military service.[1]

Around July 1938 came the notification of Eric's affidavit for America, which would allow him to leave within a few months. We rushed to Miss Schiff with the news and embraced tearfully.

On 27 April 1938, a few weeks after the Anschluss, a new law had been proclaimed: all Jews had to declare full details of their assets by 30 June that year. I remember my father's demeanour at the time, how strained, anxious and nervous he seemed. I recall him having an unusual number of meetings with lawyers, his bank manager and various anonymous officials but, at seventeen, still considered a child by my father, I was told nothing.[2]

By the autumn, many people, particularly the young, had already left Vienna, and our cousins Maxl and Leo Bodek did so in October. Having illegally entered Belgium, they sent their parents, Aunt Genya and Uncle Hermann, detailed instructions as to how to follow them, with the name of the guide who would facilitate this. I had begged my parents to let me go with them, but my cautious, upright father was fearful of doing anything unlawful.

In the meantime the event occurred which started to change his mind. On 6 November a Jew, Herschel Grynszpan, entered

49

the German embassy in Paris and shot dead Ernst vom Rath, a German diplomat.

On the night of 9 November Eric answered the telephone to our neighbours the Aments, whose apartment on the opposite side of our building overlooked Leopoldgasse and the Polnische Tempel. 'The synagogue is in flames!' one of them shouted down the line. 'Yes, yes, there are fire engines, but they are only spraying the other buildings... The SA are attacking people in the street... It's terrible... What are we going to do?' That question again.

My parents bolted the doors and turned off the lights. We crept to the window, to witness the sky burning red with the flames of what we know must be our synagogue. At midnight Kristallnacht, the Night of Broken Glass, came to our building. We heard a noise from the courtyard. Rushing to the window of our darkened home we saw Mr Hagmann talking to SA men, who then entered our building. We stepped away from the window in terror. Mother moaned, 'Will they come here? Will they come here?' And all we could do was wait and listen.

A period of silence followed, which ended with a violent crash of glass from somewhere below. A woman screamed and we heard a dull thud in the courtyard. We rushed back to the window and saw the dark shape of a person lying below. A wailing woman ran out into the courtyard and fell upon the body. Mr Hagmann emerged with the SA. Soon an ambulance arrived and took the body away.

I don't know how long we sat together in the dark, or whether we even spoke. At some point we must have simply gone to bed.

The next morning I spoke to Mr Hagmann, who wore his habitual swastika armband. 'It was Mr Epstein who died,' he told me. 'He tried to escape and jumped out of the window.' I knew the Epsteins by sight. They ran their wholesale clothing business from their first-floor apartment.

'Is that what the SA told you?' I replied, 'that a man just threw himself out of a window?'

Mr Hagmann looked down. 'Perhaps he was helped,' he murmured. Then he added, 'Some of them wanted to go higher in your building, but I told them that only an old couple lived on your floor.' On behalf of the Epsteins no such deceit had been possible. By the door of our apartment block in Untere Augartenstrasse their address plate stated: 'Robes et Modes bei Epstein.'

The embers of that terrible night were still hot the next day. Eric was in the street and saw the SA arresting Jews. One of the SA made towards him and Eric fled into our building, where he hid in a coal bunker, covering himself with as much coal as possible. Later that afternoon he ventured outside, though only to the front of our building. He was talking to a friend who wore a skullcap, when a Hitler Youth appeared from nowhere and smashed their heads together. A Christian family observed this incident and took Eric in to clean him up.

After Kristallnacht it was dangerous for Jews to walk on the streets, yet, as incredible as it seems, we still held on to the belief that order would be restored out of this insanity. But our parents' plans for our departure took on a new urgency. Eric would be leaving for America in December, and Otto was making arrangements to go to England via an illegal entry to Holland with his friend Norbert Fuchs. He could not enter Holland legally as his affidavits were not yet ready. Mr Apte from Antwerp had written to us saying he would be glad to receive me should I come to Antwerp. Perhaps this, and the terrible course of events in Austria, persuaded my father that his sons had to go, by whatever means.

My mother took me shopping to the large department store of Gerngross in Mariahilferstrasse. Winter was setting in fast but I was going to be travelling alone and partly on foot, so it was a matter of travelling as light but as warmly as possible. Mother bought gloves for me, a coat, a woollen cap with ear flaps, a coat and a rucksack. My feelings veered between anxiety and excitement. On the one hand I had no idea how I would cope without my parents' guidance or my brothers' comradeship. On the other the prospect of having nobody to tell me what to do was intoxicating. These two moods seemed to alternate, I never had them at the same time. I was either elated or anxious.

I became the first Knoller boy to leave the country of my birth, following the Bodeks into Belgium at the end of November 1938.

We stood together in our apartment, me with my rucksack and my passport with the fresh 'J' for Jew stamped on it. Into the rucksack my mother had sewn a single gold coin. 'In an emergency, you sell this,' she said to me. We were permitted to take only ten Reichsmarks out of Austria, but my father had given me another thirty, which I had secreted in my underpants.

Mother sobbed as Father took me aside. I must make right and proper decisions, he told me. Look after my health. He would then be proud that I had managed without my parents. I must write weekly, so that we remained in touch and could help one another, stay part of each other's lives, until the time we were together again. Father was fifty-six and Mother fifty-three when I left. 'You must come soon,' I begged them. My father waved aside my plea. They would not harm the old ones, he repeated, it is you young ones who are in danger. I am sure he believed this, although all our Bodek relations had already left.

'And what if things get hard here?' I asked.

'Perhaps then we will come,' said Father.

We all took the tram to the Westbahnhof. At another station, the Nordwestbahnhof, there was an antisemitic exhibition. The posters for this, displaying a caricature of a Jew with the title 'Der Ewige Jude', the letters cleverly hebraicised, were in evidence all over the city. We scarcely noticed them now. They were the norm, as were the shops we passed daubed with white Stars of David, many with large letters on their windows proclaiming: '*Kauft nicht von Juden*. Don't buy from Jews.'

Otto and Eric tried to lift our spirits. They joked with me, warning me about girls. I couldn't help swelling with pride because with their humour my elder brothers were acknowledging that I was nearly a man, like them.

My parents bought a single ticket for Cologne and then we stood on a platform, a family about to be separated by a hatred which had infected our whole country. More tears from Mother and then from me. We clung to each other for a long time. I felt only the utter, incomprehensible desolation of parting.

I stood at a compartment looking out at my family huddled together on the platform; the whistle blasted, the train jerked forward and all there was to do was to wave frantically until we had disappeared from one another's sight.

Until that journey trains had only ever been associated with holidays for me, as this was the only time we ever travelled on them. Yet my family was not beside me now and, in the heedless and quickening rhythm of the wheels, I was being carried not to some Lake Balaton and another pretty Hungarian Rosza, but to some remote city in a hostile country. How strange this was and how lost I felt. Yet that other sensation of excitement quickly took over.

I was without responsibility, accountable to no-one. I was free. Soon enough I would have my fill of such freedom, but I was never to see my parents again.

2

THE
LOST COIN

UNCLE HERMANN'S letter told us that the safest crossing point into Belgium was through Aachen. I was to proceed to a Jewish hotel, the name of which I have since forgotten, and ask for a Mr Herzgruber.

It was a slow train, taking on and disgorging hundreds of troops at almost every station. I sat as quietly as possible in the corner of a compartment, my head buried in a book. At some point a mother and her Hitler Youth son left the train. As we rattled on into the evening, the book began to feel heavy in my hand and the voices around me grew indistinct. The next thing I remember is waking up in Cologne. How relieved I felt to leave this train crammed with my enemies and breath freely again as I walked the night streets, every so often stopping to ask directions.

When I found the hotel it was swarming with people, every one of them trying to escape to somewhere. I pushed my way to the desk and asked for Mr Herzgruber. It seemed he was well known.

'Tomorrow,' I was told, 'he comes tomorrow.' I took a room and went to bed, falling asleep at once.

The next morning I met some of the refugees as we ate rolls and coffee. A young man in his twenties sat at my table. His name was Paul and he told me he was from Vienna.

'You're looking at these bruises?' he remarked. 'The bastard Nazis did it when they arrested me on Kristallnacht. They knew I was a communist, so it was three days in Dachau for me, and I'm lucky it wasn't longer. It would have been but my parents bribed the SA and they released me on condition I leave the country immediately. My parents know some quite big people in Belgium, and they've arranged entry papers for me. I'm going to collect them from the Belgian consulate here today, and I'll be in Belgium this afternoon.'

'You're lucky,' I said, 'I have to get over the border illegally.'

'How are you going to manage that?' Paul looked at me with an awkward sympathy, no doubt comparing his situation to mine.

'Some guide is going to show up and lead me across, for a fee of course.'

Herzgruber was a squat, solid man in a felt hat, every inch the German peasant. By the time I found him there were some refugees gathered around him. Others joined us, until there were four couples, as well as a girl of ten and another of about my age, both accompanying their parents. 'I'll take you to my farm,' said Herzgruber, 'it's near Aachen. From there, when it's dark, I'll get you across the border. Come now, my truck is outside.'

We climbed into the back of his covered vehicle and set off. We bumped about uncomfortably for the whole journey. Aachen is only about sixty kilometres from Cologne, but progress was slow in the old truck. When we finally stopped we were in the yard of

Herzgruber's farm. He led us to a barn. 'Until nightfall,' he said. 'Now you pay me my fee.'

'Look, you are a total stranger to us,' said someone, ' we'd be fools to hand over all of it now,' and we all murmured agreement with our spokesman. Haggling started as Herzgruber and our man attempted to reach a compromise. There was a pause as our spokesman consulted us. We tossed figures around between us, and then settled on a percentage.

'All right, it's probably too much, but we'll agree fifty per cent now and the rest when we make it across the border,' said our man. Herzgruber grumbled but agreed.

'Can you bring us food? We have a long wait until dark,' someone asked. Herzgruber nodded and later came back with bread, cheese, a few apples and coffee, for which he charged exorbitantly.

We talked among ourselves for a while and I became friendly with the parents of the younger girl. 'We are also from Vienna,' said her father, a short man in his thirties. 'Our name is Goldberg. I used to manage a jeweller's shop in Kärtner Strasse, but when the Germans came, that was the end of it. There are some people I know in Antwerp, in the diamond trade. I might find work there, make another life for all of us.'

Searching for some hope, some new shape for his shattered existence, he bore the same stolidly resigned expression which marked the faces of all the adults. They had to move on to another place, though whether that place would afford them any greater security they did not really know, and they did not choose to think about it.

'I have some contacts in Antwerp, too, also in the diamond trade,' I said. I told him about my Bodek family, who had left Vienna before Kristallnacht. 'They are in Brussels now. I am going to find them.'

57

I fell into conversation with the teenage girl, whose name I have long forgotten. I flirted mildly with her as it was my nature to do with all girls, but mostly I enjoyed talking to someone of my own age. The Goldbergs were likeable but too sober and weighed down with responsibilities for me to relate to them easily. After the girl and I had chatted about our backgrounds we admitted that we were excited about our situation and felt none of the foreboding of the adults. We glowed at the prospect of sneaking across a foreign border by night. To us it seemed a great adventure.

Eventually we fell silent and waited in the darkness for Herzgruber. Hours passed before the door swung open and I made out his dark shape, framed against a background of night. A torch flashed in his hand. 'From now on you don't talk,' he said, 'and make no noise. There are border guards everywhere. When I raise my arms like this,' and he demonstrated by lifting both arms above his head, 'you get down at once.'

We gathered our possessions and left the barn. The older girl and I exchanged glances of scarcely concealed glee in the light of the torch as we set off. Herzgruber now turned the torch off and I felt my heart race as I thought of the journey ahead. Above us glowed the light of a thin moon. I began identifying with a character in one of my trashy Tom Shark novels, about a prisoner who escaped from a South American jail.

We soon entered a forest, following Herzgruber in single file. We kept moving, twigs cracking underfoot, potholes and tree roots tripping us. At some point one of the women stumbled and let out a startled yelp of pain. Herzgruber at once raised his arms, we all hit the ground and a damp, earthy odour filled my nostrils. We lay in complete silence until our guide stood and beckoned us to move on. There were slapping sounds for a time as we brushed dirt and twigs from our clothing.

It seemed a long time before the trees started to thin out and we could walk more easily, and then Herzgruber halted and announced that we were in Belgium. We were to walk straight ahead to a small town called Verviers, about twenty-five kilometres away. There, at a hotel restaurant, we would find another guide who would take us to Brussels. We paid the remainder of the fee to Herzgruber, who counted the money carefully and then disappeared into the forest.

With our company of mixed ages it took us several hours on foot to reach Verviers. It was early morning when we arrived and, without much difficulty, found the hotel restaurant. We gave the receptionist the name of the guide, and waited. He soon appeared, arranged coffee for us and then put us in the back of another covered truck.

It was 130 kilometres to Brussels and we were exhausted and hungry when the guide deposited us at the Jewish Community Centre, a substantial building in the centre of the city. There we were given breakfast and, at last, a mattress. I fell asleep at once, but my mind gave me no rest and sent me a dream full of apprehension and insecurity. I was returning to my parents' home, they took me in their arms, I felt safe, but no, they told me I had to go at once. I protested, but it was no use, and I woke crying.

I slept again until the next afternoon, as did my comrades. We were interviewed by a senior official. What plans did I have? Did I know anyone in Belgium perhaps? I did not know it then, but in the span of two days I had been introduced to the blueprint of my life for the next five years: separation, hiding, moving, hunger, exhaustion, official questioning. 'I have an introduction to some people called Apte,' I told him, 'they are related to a neighbour and close friend of ours in Vienna. They live in Antwerp and I want to visit them. There are some of my own family, here in Brussels – refugees like me. Their name is Bodek. Can you tell me where they are? I think they must have registered.'

The official murmured. 'Yes, everyone registers with us. Wait a moment.' He dug around in some files for a while. 'Yes, this is them, I think,' he said and wrote down an address. He produced a railway ticket for Antwerp, gave me the address of the Jewish Aid Committee there and some Belgian francs. I thanked him.

I found the Bodeks living in a small apartment on the third floor of an old building. Aunt Genya cried out when she opened the door and threw her arms around me. She was my mother's sister-in-law, but so much more like her in character than Uncle Hermann, my mother's brother. Inside the sparsely furnished apartment my cousins Leo, Maxl and Rosi clustered round me in greeting. Uncle Hermann was as reserved as my father, but his expression showed that he was equally pleased to see me. Whenever I saw Uncle Hermann I always marvelled at his eyebrows, an endless source of fascination for me which exploded in a dark, lavish profusion such as I've never seen on another person. His skin was unusually dark. Altogether Uncle Hermann was a striking-looking individual.

The anxious questions started. Had I heard from my parents? What was the situation in Vienna after Kristallnacht? What had I seen? The Bodeks listened gloomily as I gave them my first-hand account of that night and its aftermath, the flames of the Polnische Tempel lighting up the night sky, the death of our neighbour Mr Epstein, the daily harassment and beating of Jews in the streets by the Brownshirts, who forced them to clean the pavements of

Vienna while jeering mobs stood watching.

My resourceful cousin Rosi had her own reasons for concern – she was trying every means to get her fiancé, Max Schächter, out of Vienna. She told me that he had been arrested after Kristallnacht and was in prison, but had managed to send her his passport. Go to any embassy, he urged her in his accompanying letter, any that would issue an entry visa, and then he could get out.

Both Maxl and Leo had found work. Leo was working with a furrier and Maxl, with whom I shared a bed that night, was tailoring. In the room stood an ironing board and large sewing machine

Even if conditions at the Bodeks' flat had not been impossibly cramped, I would not have stayed with them as my parents had insisted that I should visit the Aptes as soon as possible. 'Miss Schiff has told them all about you,' they had reminded me. Our neighbour had written their address on a piece of paper. And so the following morning I bade farewell to this splintered part of my family and set off for Antwerp by train. I followed the same routine on arrival: I made my way to the Jewish Aid Committee; a few questions, food and a mattress on the floor. As in Brussels, I was given some money – enough, I was informed, to rent a room – and instructed to return every week for a supplement.

To my delight, while I was at the Aid Committee I ran into the Goldbergs. 'Ah, Freddie!' exclaimed Mr Goldberg, 'I have a meeting tomorrow in the Diamond Club with my contact. Maybe I'll be lucky, who knows?' But I never saw the Goldbergs again.

I was advised at the Committee that it would be unwise to visit the Aptes in the evening, I never discovered why. So, next morning, unable to find their names in the telephone directory, I got directions and set off to find them. It was not far away and I enjoyed the walk, past the Pelikan Straat, with the railway station at one end and the Diamond Club – the famous and exclusive trading centre with mainly Jewish members – further along, and then past many Jewish restaurants, until I reached the Belgelei, where the Aptes lived. It was not hard to find the address from the piece of paper I had and I was soon outside their apartment block, which stood on a magnificently wide, tree-lined avenue. These Aptes were cousins of the Florida Aptes, Eric's sponsors. Success, it seemed, ran in the family.

The building was so splendid and I felt so apprehensive at arriving unannounced that I hesitated for a while before pressing the numbered button on the polished brass plate. A voice startled me, leaping out at me from a grille I had not noticed. This was my first encounter with an intercom. 'Apte,' said a female voice. I spoke into the grille, announcing my connection with Miss Schiff, not at all sure whether Mrs Apte, if it were she at the other end of the device, would know anything about me. 'Yes, yes, of course,' she said in a welcoming way, to my great relief. 'Take the lift to the fifth floor.' There was a sharp electronic buzz at the front door, which snapped ajar. I walked into the luxurious lobby, where the sound of my footsteps was instantly muffled by dense, soft carpet.

The panelled lift carried me upwards with extraordinary smoothness, the richly polished apartment doors parading slowly down before my eyes. Finally the plush apparatus slowed to a smooth, faintly sickening halt. Mrs Apte, an elegant, slim woman in her early thirties, was waiting for me at her apartment door. It was late morning, yet she still wore a robe. I was in awe before such indifference to the hour, which spoke to me of great wealth, and it is a fact that a certain diffidence on my part, born of the social gulf between the Aptes and myself, was always to characterise my

62

relationship with them. Mrs Apte did her best to put me at my ease, smiling, kissing and welcoming me in decent German before leading me into a wonderfully furnished living room. A smartly dressed maid, quite different from the country girls I had been used to in my own home, brought us coffee and biscuits on a gleaming silver tray. My hostess spoke to the maid in Flemish.

I sat awkwardly, not really knowing what to say. Eventually Mrs Apte broke the silence. 'Do you have money, Freddie?'

'Well, I have some from my parents, and the Committee, you know, they gave me some, too.'

'If you are ever in need you only have to ask.'

'Thank you very much, Mrs Apte, thank you.' But I never did take money from the Aptes. This family, who were really strangers and only connected to us through our family friendship with Miss Schiff, had already done so much for us. Mr Apte's cousin in Florida had secured papers for Eric to go there and over the time I knew the Antwerp Aptes they were a model of kindness and generosity. I could never have brought myself to take hard currency from these people.

'You must come to Friday night dinner. My husband will be here. He is away on business at present,' Mrs Apte said I readily agreed. My head was full of the magnificence of their apartment as I made my way back to the Aid Committee.

Over the next few days I fell in with a group of Viennese boys a little older than me, who seemed very streetwise. One called Walter was the leader and there was another called Paul. The three of us went looking for an apartment to share, so as to save a little of the money the Committee gave us. We found a cheap place in Leverick Straat, in the heart of the Orthodox Jewish quarter. The smell of chickens and their droppings revolted me. Orthodox Jews

63

with beards and kaftans ran the shops and I could see them butchering animals in the kosher way.

Walter and Paul seemed determined to corrupt me, or, as they would have put it, to educate me. 'Come on, Freddie, have a little drink. What's the matter with it? You need to loosen up. We'll teach you poker... You'll have fun.'

They gambled with some of the other refugees, and when they taught me poker I lost heavily to them. It was not the week's allowance I had to hand over to them that remains such a painful memory; no, it was the forfeit of the gold coin which my mother had sewn into the lining of my rucksack. My gambling debt was 'the emergency' that parted me from a mother's loving thought.

Then the boys taught me whoring. First they took me to the dock area, to a narrow street where the prostitutes leaned half naked from windows, calling raucously to passers-by. It was the first time I had ever seen a woman's bare breasts. I saw sailors entering the dark passageways below their windows. The boys laughed and I pretended not to be shocked by what I saw. Slightly less shocking were the prostitutes who frequented a bistro opposite the railway station. The boys went with them regularly. 'Come on, Freddie, why not try?' they urged me. I knew I would be judged by Walter and Paul if I did not go through with it, and I dreaded their judgement.

It was my first complete sexual experience. I veered between desire and disgust as I stood in the dingy room with the prostitute I had selected. I was fascinated by her breasts, and when I touched them I had an erection, and put on the condom she gave me, but I was also thinking of all the men she had been with. The woman dealt swiftly with my uncertainties and got on top of me. I ejaculated, dressed, and was out of the door. The boys descended on me outside in the street, harrying me with questions. I told them how great it had all been and invented, with some fluency, all sorts of details about what she did to my penis with her mouth and tongue. They listened wide-eyed. My fabrications came from a pornographic booklet I had read, which my father had discovered and, of course, destroyed.

The end of my relationship with the boys came when they brought beer and wine into the house and we spent the night drinking heavily. I vomited, was laid up for a whole day and could not eat for another two. When I recovered, I was disgusted with myself. This was what I was making of my new freedom. I thought of my father's parting words about how I should conduct myself to make him proud of me. I kept seeing my parents' faces before me, filled with expressions of sad reproach. It was an unendurable picture. All I had wanted to do was keep up with the boys, to be more of a man, as I imagined they were, and all I had become was a mockery of a man. I could not continue in this way. It was enough. There were no hard feelings. 'If you want to go, that's fine,' said Walter, and we all parted on good terms. We were just from different worlds, that was all.

Among the throng of refugees I soon found a boy of my own age who needed someone to share his room. I told him what I had been doing and how ashamed of myself I was, and he invited me to share with him. Kurt was a pale, shy, gently spoken boy from Vienna, though I cannot recall his family name. He did not share my obsession with the opposite sex and at night he sometimes wept with homesickness. I felt on safe ground again. He rented a clean, tidy room in a gentile neighbourhood from Flemish people, who sometimes invited us for dinner. I was happy there.

Then there was my standing invitation to the Aptes for Friday-night dinner, which soon became the highlight of my week. It was a blessing to feel part of a family again. Mr Apte was a tall, urbane man. His soft voice and Flemish pronunciation made it difficult for me to understand his German, so I spent a lot of time smiling and nodding in a show of comprehension. He loved classical music and often, after dinner, we would sit in front of his gramophone and listen to symphonies. Instead of the money I would not take from them, the Aptes gave me presents, once a tie and a pullover and, quite often, bars of chocolate.

Jos Apte was an important member of the Antwerp Diamond Club, and his business colleagues would often join us for dinner. I listened politely to their conversation, and would have been out of my depth even if I had understood their rapid French. The Aptes were modern, highly cultivated people who, while maintaining their Jewish identity, attended synagogue only on high holidays. They had a child, a boy of about four years old, cared for by a resident nanny, who would come in to be with his mother and would play with us for a while before being taken off to bed.

During that first Friday-night dinner the Aptes plied me with questions about the situation in Austria. Once again I described the terrifying events at home. Mr Apte suggested I might like to call my parents, and I leapt at the opportunity, while expressing dismay about the cost of such a call. He dismissed my concern.

I stood beside Mr Apte as he made all the necessary international connections with the operator. Then he passed the handset to me and I trembled as I heard the ringing tone in our apartment in Vienna. It was my mother who answered, calling 'Hello! Hello!' All I could manage to say was, 'It's me, Freddie!' before I broke down. *'Mein Kind! Mein Kind! Wo bist du?'* she called down the line. 'Where are you speaking from? Please! Say something!' Mrs Apte took the telephone from me and spoke quietly to my mother while I struggled to control myself. Finally I signalled that I was able to speak again. After I had talked with my mother, my father came on the line, his voice breaking with emotion, and then Otto, who told me he was soon leaving for England with his friend Norbert Fuchs. Next to speak was Miss Schiff, who was Mr Apte's cousin. I broke down again and once more Mrs Apte took over. I was surprised to hear her talking in French, because I did not know that Miss Schiff spoke the language.

'Freddie, you can call your family every Friday,' said Mr Apte. 'And please don't worry about the cost.' Joy at speaking to my parents mingled with all the feelings of homesickness their voices stirred up in me.

I had received a letter from my parents at the beginning of December 1938 telling me of Eric's departure for America, and one from Otto in January 1939 about a failed attempt to get into Holland. The Dutch had arrested him and his companions, put them in prison for the night and deposited them at the border the next morning with orders to walk back to Germany. Something had made Otto fall behind his companions and when, some hours later, he did cross the border, a guard told him that his companions had been arrested by the SS.[1] From my parents came a further letter, telling me that everything was fine, that Father was still working for Grossner & Weiss, and a suggestion that I get in touch with a distant relative by the name of Adolph Menashes, who lived in Cairo, in Rue Antikhana. Apparently he was a music professor at the academy there. I didn't even know we had relatives in Cairo, but I wrote to him and he replied enclosing £2 in £1 sterling notes. Every month from then on a letter came from him, enclosing the same amount – a large sum for me.

My parents had written to tell me that my cello was on its way, and it was with great excitement that I collected it from a depot in Antwerp in January 1939. It had been sent via a regular Austrian shipping agent, so my parents must have gained permission from the authorities to dispatch it.[2] I sometimes took it along to the Aptes', where my hostess accompanied me on the piano.

On one occasion the Aptes invited me to go for a weekend to a very smart resort on the Belgian coast called Knokke. What a sensation it was to sit in the back of their big American car. In the front the Aptes chatted non-stop. Every so often they would address a few words to me in German so that I wouldn't feel ignored. But I didn't mind being forgotten, because this trip was such a delight. I just liked being in the car and looking out of the window. Nobody I had ever known before had owned a car, let alone an American one. Just to take a taxi was a real extravagance for us. At the doors of the imposing hotel an army of smart, po-faced porters greeted us and took our luggage. I had a marvellous room and was so enthralled with the scale of the adjoining bathroom that I whiled away a lot of time just luxuriating in the steaming water. Breakfast on the Saturday morning was something of an ordeal for me, simply because I wanted to eat everything in sight at the wonderful buffet, but was embarrassed to appear a glutton in front of the Aptes. So, the next morning, I forsook the luxury of my room and came down early to have my fill of the delicious offerings.

We travelled along the coast that weekend, through Blankenberge and Ostend, and in these and the other smaller resorts I enjoyed being among the crowd of holidaymakers, whose easy, carefree manner almost persuaded me that the world was still a safe place. We ate at splendid restaurants, and it was at one of these that the Aptes introduced me to seafood, for they were not, as I have said, observant Jews. A plate of shrimps was set before each of us and I gazed uncertainly at the pink, black-eyed carcasses, quite willing to eat this new delicacy but unsure how to. I looked on in astonishment as the Aptes used their fingers to peel away the segmented outer crust of the shrimp. I had been brought up to believe that to eat at table in this manner was the height of bad manners. Still I followed suit, feeling I had learnt something new and interesting about social customs. The shrimps tasted of the sea, fresh and tangy, and I found them very agreeable.

I noticed a lot of refugees working in our hotel. I fell into conversation with a uniformed Jewish waiter, who I remember spoke what seemed to me to be quite good French. 'They always need people in the summer,' he told me. 'There's lots of us working in the kitchens.'

That summer I spoke to Kurt about going to Knokke. 'It's a great place,' I said, 'and we can get work there.' We hitch-hiked. And so, once again, I got to stay in one of those smart hotels, the Regent, but this time in a small dormitory for casual summer workers. With no Flemish and little French, it was dishwashing for Kurt and me. The work was hard, the pay adequate, but the food excellent. In our free time we mingled with young people in the town and on the beach, boasting that we were guests at the Regent. Sometimes we went to clubs to meet girls, and danced till late, but none of this resulted in more than friendly chat with them.

When Kurt and I returned from Knokke, in August, we went as usual to collect our weekly allowance from the Jewish Aid Committee. One of the organisers was direct with me: 'Money is short here. We're flooded with refugees. You simply have to move on.' I was allocated to the Merksplas camp, near Mechelen, and lost contact with Kurt. This turned out to be a very agreeable place. I slept in a dormitory with other refugees.

The camp was near the Belgian-Dutch border, about thirty kilometres from Antwerp. There were two large brick buildings, Pavilions A and B, each housing about a hundred and sixty refugees. Each dormitory – there were four to a pavilion – slept forty. There was also an administration building, and a building where courses in metalwork, poster making, shoe repairing, blacksmithing and tailoring were offered. I did a little tailoring, but spent most of my time practising with the orchestra.

Merksplas marked the end of my happy visits to the Aptes. Being a camp, it had its regime: one had to spend every night there. Besides, it was a difficult and expensive journey to Antwerp from there, even if I had gained permission. The Aptes were sad, but said it was very important that I do whatever the Committee required of me.

Troubles for my parents continued to cause me grave anxiety. My father informed me in a letter around this time that he had left Grossner & Weiss, his job for as long as I could remember, and was now working for the Kultusgemeinde, the Jewish Community Centre.[3]

August 1939 saw the signing of the non-aggression pact between Hitler and Stalin, and at Merksplas, where we listened to the German radio and had access to newspapers, we speculated whether this would mean that Hitler would turn his gaze westwards. 'Perhaps we should try to get to England, put water between us and the Germans,' said some. 'France, that's where I'll go,' said others, 'the Maginot Line is impregnable.' But all of us felt again the cold grasp of insecurity. When Germany invaded Poland on 1 September, everyone was convinced that France and Belgium would be next. Two days later Britain and France declared war on Germany and we knew that all we could do was wait for the time when we would have to flee.

I received a letter from my parents in which they told me that the American consulate had no record of their application for visas. It was distressing in the extreme to read this news, as I was helpless to do anything for them.[4]

Another letter I received following the German invasion of Poland was even more upsetting. My father was a meticulous individual, who would never allow a crossing out to appear in a letter he wrote. Yet around the time I was at Merksplas I received just such a letter and the deletion in it drew my attention at once. The line was straight and fine and did not obscure the words beneath.[5] Father had written:

'Many are ~~now being forced to go~~ returning to the country where I was born.'

Of course I knew that Jews had been deported to Poland – it was this policy of 'repatriation' that had led to the assassination of vom Rath in Paris, the excuse for the Kristallnacht pogrom. I understand that my father was communicating his fear that this might be his and my mother's fate.

Through the Jewish Community Centre in Brussels I had made contact with some Jewish musicians. They played at weddings and other functions. I had made a little money playing cello at two wedding receptions. Once, I played at a nightclub. A bass musician had fallen ill, and another musician asked me if I could stand in. I jumped at the opportunity. I couldn't play bass, but told him I could. I thought I could muddle through, especially as I knew I would not need a bow for jazz. I had sometimes improvised jazz

71

tunes with Otto and Eric in Vienna.

The ground floor of Pavilion A was used as the concert hall and theatre. Here, the Merkplas orchestra rehearsed. There were about fifteen of us in the orchestra and, although we had string players, I was the only cellist. There was a saxophonist, a couple of clarinettists and a trumpeter. We made do. We had a very good pianist as a soloist and not a bad concert grand piano. The conductor, a professional called Peter Mautner, was from Vienna. Professional Belgian musicians made up our numbers for any special concert and it was very pleasurable for all the refugees when they joined us for rehearsals and the augmented sound produced by these fine players filled the hall. The concerts were usually fund-raising affairs for the Jewish Aid Committee in Antwerp or Brussels and sometimes we went to those cities to perform for this purpose.

But I wasn't at Merksplas for long. 'This country is flooded with refugees,' one of the directors told me. 'We want you to go to Eksaarde. Everyone under twenty-one has to go there. It won't be bad. There is an orchestra, and I hear they need cellos.' So, in February 1940, that is where I went.

Eksaarde, an old military bastion with red-brick barracks, was near Ghent. The dormitories were small – four refugees slept in each room. The place was run by a German Catholic who had fled his home because he was in danger of arrest for his anti-Nazi views.

The orchestra at Eksaarde was inferior to that of Merksplas because all the players were young, but still I enjoyed playing there. Rehearsals were twice a week, and we performed for a refugee audience every weekend. Sometimes members of the Jewish organisations which sponsored us would be invited to attend, in order to maintain their support.

So I waited on events, and they soon overtook us. On the morning of 10 May 1940 the relative peace of Eksaarde ended with a scream of sirens wrenching us from sleep. The radio told us that the German invasion of Belgium had begun.

With no warning at all of the invasion, panic followed. We were hastily assembled, and sorted into groups of ten. 'Make your own way – to Ostend, or to France. We cannot advise you because we know no more than you. Take only essentials!' My cello was not an essential, but how I hated leaving it behind! With its loss, I felt I was leaving part of myself, the part which tied me to my life in Vienna, to my parents. When I played I always thought of home, of them, of the Knoller trio.

We were warned not to talk, and told that the newspapers were full of stories of fifth columnists and that we, as German speakers, would fall under suspicion. And so we set out on foot towards France, a three-hour walk away, comforting ourselves that we would be safe behind the great defences of the Maginot Line.

The roads leading to France were crammed with a crawling mass of refugees. Family cars and wagons, filled with every conceivable possession, jammed the roads, making progress slow. I was glad to be unencumbered and on foot, able to move relatively easily and swiftly, but nobody had expected the sudden appearance of a German plane, which dived out of the air and strafed us. Those of us on foot tumbled into ditches, but many of the laden vehicles were destroyed. 'Can't they see we are civilians?' people cried to one another incredulously. I walked on blindly, oblivious to the injured and dead. We shared a single idea: let us only get to France.

An hour or so later we reached Tournai, a town near the French border. I was with another boy from Eksaarde. Belgian and Jewish refugees alike thronged the station, in the hope of catching a train to France, or perhaps even to the coast, where there might be a boat to England. It didn't matter – whatever train arrived we would take it. But, as we stood waiting in our hundreds, the dismal howl of sirens erupted again. An air raid followed almost immediately. My companion and I looked around desperately for somewhere to hide and then, despite the confusion, I spotted a large concrete tube. We flung ourselves down and crawled into it as the bombs, screaming horribly through the air, rained down and exploded. From this hiding place I had a keyhole view of the chaos outside. I was in terror and I am not ashamed to say that I wet myself. I saw a whole section of the station engulfed in flames. It seemed a long time before the all-clear sounded. We crawled out into a scene of devastation, coughing as our lungs filled with the choking dust of pulverised masonry. In place of the terrible noise of the bombs we now heard something more dreadful, the moans of pain and screams of women. One woman wandered in a daze, calling out for her family. Whether she found any of them, I shall never know.

Another boy from Eksaarde stumbled upon us and, choking and shaking, the three of us left this scene of destruction.[6] As the air cleared we saw bodies, whole and dismembered, lying in pools of blood. I vomited what little food I had in me.

3

WEATHERING THE STORM

THERE HAD been no controls at the Belgian border with France, but as our straggling mass reached the outskirts of Lille, the first large French town, we came upon a solid blue cordon of French police. Everyone was asked for identification. Belgian citizens were allowed to pass. We three boys showed our passports, embossed with the large red 'J'. The police called an officer. *'Nous Juive refugies. Hitler,'* we said in our pidgin French. They didn't seem to understand. Pointlessly, we repeated the words louder. All the police saw were German passports and so they arrested and handcuffed us as enemy aliens. At a nearby police station a German-speaking policeman separated us and interrogated us individually. I explained my history in a rush of words. He asked me to show him my penis to prove I was a Jew. I had a feeling that this officer was a Jew himself. He said he believed my story. 'You are going to a place where you will be cared for,' he assured me. My two friends had the same experience with this officer.

Guarded by soldiers, we slept on straw in a crowded room in a school building. Inside were other German speakers. It was obvious by their demeanour, dress, and the way they kept themselves apart that they were not Jews but fifth columnists. I remember meeting a Hungarian who had a German passport. It was a confused situation.

The next day we assembled in a courtyard and were then marched through the streets under guard. People shouted *'Sales Boches!* Dirty Krauts!' and a woman emptied a piss pot over us from an upper window.

Where were we going? Of course, nobody could answer this question. About all we knew was that it was the month of June. We were escorted to a station, on to a platform and loaded on to cattle trucks, with barbed wire over the narrow openings. Cattle trucks; this was my first experience of travelling in one, and by no means the worst. Refugees and fifth columnists separated into opposing groups. There were about ten of us and twenty of them and they, German Nazis, continually taunted us. A typically blond young one boasted, 'Germany will easily conquer France,' and added, 'You Jews will be sorted out soon enough.' It would have been foolish to pick a fight with the numbers so against us and the conditions so cramped, so I confined myself to a neutral response, along the lines of 'let's wait and see what the future brings'.

At least we slept on straw in this cattle truck and the train stopped twice a day, in the middle of nowhere, when French soldiers distributed food: some bread and cheese. They provided a metal cup, which we dipped into a bucket full of water and allowed us, under their guns, to climb out and relieve ourselves in the fields.

After two days the train stopped. The sign said 'St Cyprien', but at first I thought I must be dreaming, because when the doors rolled back and my eyes adjusted to the blinding sun the scene which greeted me was from a holiday postcard – a deep-blue sea and a silver beach. But no, there to the right were barbed wire and watchtowers. We were led inside the camp and cheerily greeted with waves from other detainees. Fine sand blew everywhere.

St Cyprien, some ten kilometres from Perpignan, was an internment camp, originally used for refugees from the Spanish Civil War of a few years before. Now we were to be interned there as enemy aliens. The camp was guarded by Sudanese soldiers.

As soon as we arrived we were led to a large assembly hall where a French officer addressed the new arrivals – about sixty of us. 'All of you are enemies of France. Any attempt at escape is punishable by death.' This dire threat of the ultimate penalty may have been no more than fine words to impress us, for it soon became clear that escape from the camp was a relatively easy matter. We were escorted to barracks, where the Jews among us found ourselves again among the German fifth columnists. Aggressively they sang their German marching songs and boasted that Hitler would soon liberate them, which, for all the idiocy of their ranting, was a true enough prediction. The Jews responded that Hitler would never win the war. The Germans hurled the word 'Jews!' at us and we shouted 'Nazis!' at them. Fights broke out.

A delegation of Jews, of which I was a member, went to the camp commandant two days later to demand to be housed separately from the Germans. Our spokesman, who spoke perfect French, declared that we would never submit to sharing barracks with the Nazis who had persecuted us in Germany. Eventually the officer yielded to our request, perhaps as much for the orderly administration of his camp as for any humanitarian reasons. We now saw the Nazis only at roll call or when we ate.

There were between one and two thousand prisoners at St Cyprien, separated from the Mediterranean by the barbed wire. Hygiene hardly existed, so diarrhoea ran riot throughout the camp and, in addition, we were tormented by lice. All day long we sat around, talking in a desultory way about the military situation or, for amusement, playing a game which consisted of nothing more than throwing a stone at a line drawn in the sand. I wondered about but never again saw my two companions from Eksaarde.

We speculated about a strange monolith on the beach, a large, low slab of concrete serving no apparent purpose. Soon we discovered that under it were the bodies of thousands of Spanish Republican refugees who had died during a cholera outbreak while interned at the camp. I needed no further evidence that I had to escape from this place. Once a week a path was cleared through the barbed wire so that we could briefly bathe in the warm sea. This was the event of the week for us, but the soldiers' guns were always on us and all too soon we were forced from the delights of the water.

I wrote and sent cards to my parents, who were frantic about my whereabouts, and to Eric.[1]

Remarkably I can barely recall my relatives being at St Cyprien. I can therefore say little about them over this period. I know that I had been at the camp scarcely two months when my cousin Rosi arrived, and I was to discover she was a very strong-willed and resourceful woman. She was intent on getting her husband Max Schächter out – they had married in Belgium – and made a real nuisance of herself. First she developed heatstroke and they sent her to the camp infirmary to recover. The camp commandant then wanted her to leave, but she steadfastly refused – unless Max was allowed to leave with her. As she was able to prove that Max would not be a burden on the state because she could provide for him, the commandant agreed to release him. This success encouraged Leo to negotiate for his father's release. He succeeded, because Leo's passport proved he was born in Switzerland. The commandant washed his hands of all of them, and finally I was the only member of the family to remain. Leo took me aside just before departing. 'Look, you know it's not very hard to escape from here. We'll all meet in Gaillac,' he said, handing me a scrap of paper with the address.

One day a Sudanese guard, a particularly big man, beckoned to me. I went over to him and he offered me a piece of chocolate. 'Come,' he said, 'I have more in my quarters.' I was an innocent nineteen-year-old, and looked even younger. I couldn't believe my luck: a delicacy like chocolate could be exchanged for a lot of food. We went to the guardhouse, which was deserted. He led me to his room, where he showed me a big bar of chocolate. He handed this to me and, before I knew what was happening, he had grabbed me and started fondling my private parts. I struggled and then struck him in the eye with the only weapon to hand, namely the chocolate bar. He let go, and, shocked and disgusted, I kneed him in the groin and ran for my life. When I got back to my barracks I was dismayed to discover that I did not even have the chocolate.

A young Viennese called Sigi, who had arrived with me on the same train from Orléans, worked in the infirmary. 'Listen, there are cholera cases here,' he confided, and I thought of the concrete slab on the beach. It was all too much. I feared retaliation from the Sudanese guard, and now there was this. I invited a boy of my own age to join me in an escape, but he refused, so I made up my mind to go alone.

The soldiers were becoming uneasy around this time. It was clear that something was in the air and we soon heard on the grapevine that France had fallen. The armistice was signed on 22 June 1940 in the railway carriage at Compiègne. The Nazi detainees were released from St Cyprien, and only the Jews remained. Because St Cyprien was in the Unoccupied Zone of France, it fell under the control of the Vichy government, formed on 11 July.

When I made my escape, one night in mid August, it proved as easy as Leo had predicted. I simply crawled under some loose barbed wire. The war was over for France, so perhaps we were more trouble than we were worth to the camp authorities.

In the pitch-darkness I kept looking nervously over my shoulder. A little later I heard the sound of an approaching vehicle, the lights of a car shone around the corner and I threw myself down until it was dark again. I reached the outskirts of Perpignan, found a concealed spot in a wood and fell asleep at once. I dreamt of the Sudanese soldier. He was pursuing me, clutching chocolate bars in his hands. I woke just as he reached out to seize me.

It was a fiercely hot, bright day, and I heard the sounds of busy traffic. I stood up, but with no clear idea of what to do. I was alone and very hungry, but all I had was a little Belgian money. I walked into Perpignan and wandered around aimlessly for a while, weak from hunger and the gathering heat of the city. I was trusting in a miracle, and then a miracle happened. I saw a group of boy scouts. I had been a boy scout in Vienna and so I knew the international greeting. I approached the boys, saluted them in the prescribed manner and explained in broken French that I had fled

Vienna when the Nazis marched in because I was a Jew. I was hungry, I told them, and had no money. Could they help me? Perhaps, for once, looking young for my age was an advantage, because one of the boys stepped forward. 'Come with me,' he said. He parted from his friends and soon we were walking down a tree-lined avenue. Roger, for that was his name, was talking animatedly, but I could pick up only the odd word or two, which seemed to be about scouting. I just nodded and gave an occasional murmur to show I was listening, while all the time my stomach growled. Soon Roger was leading me up the drive of one of the elegant houses lining the avenue. I hovered at a polite distance as he spoke in a low voice with his parents at the front door and gestured towards me. His parents followed his gaze, looking concerned. I was about to experience the kindness of strangers. Roger's mother beckoned to me, embraced me as if I were her own son and took me into the wonderfully cool interior of the handsome house. She sat me down and before long returned with a tray laden with an omelette, orange juice, coffee, jam, bread and butter. It was a feast I remember to this day, though at the time I was too hungry to appreciate its taste. When I had finished, Roger's parents came to talk with me. What was I going to do? they wanted to know.

'I need to get to Gaillac, I have family there,' I explained.

'Stay with us for now. We'll sort your ticket out.' They clearly saw how tired I was and insisted I lay down on a couch. I fell asleep immediately. When I woke later that day I felt awkward because I had no way of repaying these kind people. How good it would have been to have stayed there with them! I managed to make them understand that I had to leave, to find my family. They nodded understandingly. Roger's mother gave me a packet of fruit and sandwiches for my journey and kissed me goodbye. I shook hands with his father. Roger himself accompanied me to the station, where he bought my ticket. We embraced and I promised to remain in touch. I didn't. What a pleasure, what a luxury that would have been. But keeping in touch is for those who have a home or at least some picture of their own future. I had neither of these consoling certainties. Yet, to this day, I feel guilty that I did not send those good people even a note of thanks.

I arrived in Gaillac, some 250 kilometres from Perpignan, at dusk. Unoccupied France was full of refugees and Gaillac, a medium-sized town in the *département* of Tarn, was no exception. In my halting French I got directions to the Bodeks' house. And what an unexpected pleasure the sight of it proved to be, with its urns of flowers set in a well-tended front garden. Aunt Genya cried with joy on seeing me, but I could not help but notice how much older she looked and how haggard and anxious Uncle Hermann was. We all lived under the strain of uncertainty, but at their age this violent upheaval must have taken a terrible toll. The question that hung perpetually over us was: what might tomorrow bring? Still, there was some comfort to be gained from further proof of Cousin Rosi's strength of character and remarkable initiative. 'How did you manage to get here,' I asked her.

'Mama and I were in a camp for women quite near St Cyprien, but I bribed a guard to let us out and we came here, then went to get Papa out of St Cyprien.' Max Schächter listened as we spoke. He was a much less determined character altogether than Rosi, and it was she who – with a little luck – had been instrumental in springing him from an Austrian jail after Kristallnacht.

Max now elaborated on the few facts Rosi had given me in Belgium. 'The reason they arrested me was because I was Polish,' he told me. 'When I wrote to Rosi, she sent me a registered letter and it was her idea for me to send her my passport.'

'I was making arrangements to get him a visa to Santo Domingo, in South America,' Rosi interjected.

'Somehow, whether they thought the letter was the visa, I don't know,' Max continued, 'but they looked at it and gave me twenty-four hours to leave the country. So Rosi and I were together in Belgium.'

A period of calm followed and in forgetful moments it was almost possible to think normality had returned to our lives. Pitchfork in hand, I worked on the top of a wagon for a farmer.

It was in Gaillac that I purchased my very first set of forged papers. Unsurprisingly, business in their production was brisk. For 100 francs, some Jewish refugees told me, you could buy some sort of identification card with your photo on it and the tricolour, which looked quite official. The town's Jewish Community Centre distributed small sums of money to refugees and when I had managed to save 100 francs I bought a card from a Frenchman in a bistro. It looked grand. The heading proudly declared *'Sauveteur Médaillé'*, and a replica of the medal and the tricolour were emblazoned on the page, next to my photograph. My new name was Robert Metzner and my new place of birth, Metz. Underneath, in small printed letters, was a declaration that the holder had saved a person from drowning. I felt sure the document would fool any German. I did not even consider whether it might fool the French authorities, who were not the enemy as far as I was concerned.

I was soon restless. An idea was forming in my mind, absurd, foolhardy, but irresistible. I would go back into occupied Belgium to find Maxl and rescue my cello. Leo was desperate to find his brother, convinced he was still in Brussels. But in my mind another, secret agenda was forming, which had little to do with cellos. Paris, city of my dreams, beautiful Paris, yes, but also licentious Paris, was a city tantalisingly close to Brussels. It mattered nothing to me that the Germans occupied it.

We were homeless and above all, paperless, that worst of all situations. All I had were my false documents and passport with a 'J' stamped on it. Leo was somewhat better off because although he held, after the Anschluss, a German passport, he had been born in Switzerland, a neutral country, so obtaining a *laissez-passer* was easy for him, and he was likely to be safer than me in an occupied country.

Insecurity was our daily bread. We were all on the run, so that no one idea seemed any more foolhardy than any other. But, despite our precarious position, unoccupied France was a far safer place for Jews than occupied Belgium. Uncle Hermann and Aunt Genya raged at us when we announced our intentions. 'Are you *meshugga*? Going into the lion's den like this... How can you think of doing it?'

Leo left for Brussels and I followed a few weeks later, having managed to obtain a *laissez-passer* from the Mairie, the town hall, in Gaillac by showing my papers declaring me to be from Alsace, which been annexed by the Germans. I told them I wanted to be reunited with my parents in my home town of Metz.

The demarcation line between Occupied and Vichy France was at Limoges. The Jewish Community Centre in Gaillac did, at this time, communicate with Vichy, and passes could be obtained in this way.

When my train arrived in Brussels I went straight to Maxl's address, and found both him and Leo well. Maxl had, of course, been separated from his family, who had fled when the Germans invaded and he had been at Eksaarde. He told me how he had tried to get to England via Middelkirk. 'That German Catholic in charge there led us – what a brave man he was – but disappeared on the way in all the chaos. None of us knew what happened to him.' I told Maxl about my time at St Cyprien, not forgetting the episode of the Sudanese guard and the chocolate bar.

Next I made my way to Antwerp – there was a fast bus service from Brussels – to see the Aptes. There was no answer when I pushed the intercom button which had so impressed me a year before. I found the caretaker. 'You won't find them, they are gone, they left before the Germans invaded,' he told me. Just one year on, and now everything had changed. I was gripped by a sense of foreboding, by a terror of the impermanence of things. Had it all been a dream? The elegant Aptes, their beautiful apartment, the Friday evenings, the trip to Knokke in their fabulous car? Couldn't even they, with all their wealth and status, have done anything against the tide of events? No, they were gone, as if they never had lived here, but the building remained and I wished that it, too, were gone, because its survival made me feel hollow.

From there I made my way to the famous Diamond Club in Pelikan Straat. These were the early years of the war, and the Jewish community still functioned in relative freedom in France and Belgium. 'Jos Apte? They all went to England,' the dealers told me. For these dealers it was business as usual and I still wonder at the fate of these less far-sighted people. They were curious about me and when I told them my story they referred me to the Jewish Community Centre, which again bailed me out with some money, food and a place to lodge.[2] The very next day I travelled to Eksaarde, only to find it deserted and ransacked. Nothing remained.

How sad I was that I could not find my cello. This seemed far more important than the fact that I was in a country occupied by my enemies. It was as if the last tie to my home – those Knoller trio evenings after Sabbath dinner, the charity performances with my mother looking on with pride – had been obliterated in the pillage. I was utterly adrift and homesick.[3]

I made my way back to Brussels, bought a ticket for Paris and changed my few remaining Belgian for French francs. I was thrilled to be going at last to the mythical city of night-twinkling boulevards, tucked-away bistros and, above all, high-kicking show girls.

4

ESCORTING
THE ENEMY

IT WAS an uneventful journey, but as soon as I passed through the ticket barrier at the Gare du Nord I saw German personnel wherever I looked, among them the black-uniformed SS and leather-coated Gestapo. I immediately followed the signs for the Métro.

How impressive the large Métro concourse was, with its hurrying crowds. In Vienna we had just one, not very busy underground line, the Stadtbahn, which ran along the Danube, whereas here I stood in front of a plan displaying an intricate network of criss-crossing lines marked with hundreds of stations, confirming that I was in a great city. I did not have to think about my destination; I already knew it. It was Montmartre, whose fame I knew from my schooldays, when we had all talked about the Folies Bergère and the Moulin Rouge and knew that girls danced half naked in these places. It was hard to believe that I was actually plotting my journey there, rather than just dreaming about it. Of course I had no idea where it was, but as I tried to find it on the plan someone came along, pushed some buttons and a snake path of lights came on, displaying a route. What an ingenious system! I thought. I followed suit and the lights showed that Montmartre and the red-light district of Pigalle were just a few stations away.

During the short journey I sat in a half dream, excited but still disbelieving, taking in my fellow passengers with a tourist's curiosity. Soon I stood at the top of the Métro station's steps, Montmartre all around me. I asked for directions for the Folies Bergère. It was not far away, in Rue Richer.

A grand building, it was more like a theatre than a cabaret, with its imposing white façade and glass-panelled doors. In front of it was a sight I had never seen in Vienna, nor in any other city: showcases filled with photographs of topless dancing girls kicking out their shapely legs, displayed right here, on a public street. I simply could not take my eyes away from them.

Soon enough, though, their attraction waned as my stomach started to grumble. I turned away and was surprised to see around me many restaurants showing the Star of David. I had stumbled across what was obviously a Jewish district. Right next door to the Folies Bergère was a restaurant called Chez Huberman. I was starving, penniless and lonely, and here before me was a reminder of who and what I was.

Instead of all the hatred and destruction in Vienna, here in Paris a Jew was apparently not yet afraid to be a Jew. I went into the pleasant courtyard in which the restaurant stood, hopeful of finding some charity. Seeing no one about, I ventured inside, and found myself in a large, attractive room with an extravagant vase of flowers on a stand and tables laid with white tablecloths and sparkling cutlery for the evening trade. It all made me feel even hungrier. Moments later a short, round woman appeared, her head framed with a mass of greying curls. I was reassured at once, for here was a woman every inch the Yiddisher mamma.

'*Bonjour*. What can I do for you, young man?' she asked, smiling warmly. Her air of proprietorship left me in no doubt that she was the owner of the place, Mrs Huberman.

My French was not fluent, but somehow I made myself understood. I explained that I was a Jewish refugee. 'I am from Vienna... My name is Freddie Knoller,' I said, having no fears here about disclosing my real name. 'I saw the Magen David on your restaurant... I have no money... I am hungry.'

Mrs Huberman looked at me sympathetically. '*Kannst du reddn Yiddish?* Can you speak Yiddish?'

'*Ja*,' I replied, '*aber mein Yiddish is a mishmash Deutsch und Yiddish*.'

She beckoned me to follow her, then called to someone out of sight, 'Otto! Otto!', and a young man appeared, as if he had been waiting for such a signal. 'Otto! This is another young man from Vienna.'

Otto, whose surname was Geringer, shook me by the hand and embraced me. He looked very young, about my own age, with thick-rimmed glasses, dark hair and brown eyes, and a prominent nose. Studious and Jewish-looking was how I saw him. 'I am from the ninth district,' he said. I was at the Chajes Gymnasium.' This was a well-known Jewish school. 'My parents, they are still in Vienna. They got me out... But tell me about yourself.'

'I lived right near you, in the second district. I went to the Sperl Gymnasium,' I began, but just then Mrs Huberman, who had disappeared while we were talking, appeared bearing a bowl of steaming chicken soup and a leg of boiled chicken, which I knew as a *pulke*.

'You must sit and eat,' she said.

Despite my sharp appetite, I shed tears. It was the smell of the food, I think, which overcame me. 'Mrs Huberman,' I said, 'this is the food my mother makes, and I have no idea when I might see her again.' Mrs Huberman set the tray down and embraced me. Perhaps Otto had been just as lost as me when he first arrived.

When I had recovered myself and eaten something, I told them how I had left Austria and entered Belgium. 'Yes, like you, my parents got me out,' I told Otto. 'Have you been in France long?' I asked him.

'Before the Germans invaded. I came straight here, soon after Kristallnacht. I have some family contacts in France, but now it is a different situation here, of course. Tell me, did your parents follow you?'

I explained that my story was much the same as his, but when I went into detail about how I had come to be in Paris my listeners' looks of interest turned to puzzled dismay. They repeated my own words back to me, as if they could not be sure they had heard me correctly. 'You are saying you went back to Belgium from the Unoccupied Zone to find your cousin … or for a cello? And then just decided to come here, to Paris?'

I added, feeling somewhat sheepish now, that it had always been a dream of mine to see Paris. 'The Eiffel Tower, the Champs-Élysées, the lights, all those places.' I said. Out of respect for Mrs Huberman I omitted the main part of my Parisian fantasy.

'Perhaps you might have waited for a better time, young man,' she remarked. 'You were really crazy to come here, you know, I don't understand you at all.'

There was little I could say in response. I scarcely understood my behaviour myself. Only that it had something to do with escape, because everything in my life had changed for ever. As

Otto had said, 'now it is a different situation'.

'What papers do you have?' Mrs Huberman asked me. I produced them: my German passport with the large red 'J' stamped across it, my bogus French papers bearing the tricolour and the name Robert Metzner.

Mrs Huberman shook her head in dismay once again. 'The gendarmes here in this district won't be fooled by these papers for a second,' she said, smacking her hand against the French ones. 'They come here all the time, checking and snooping, and they are taking all the non-French away.' She glanced anxiously at Otto. 'They've always been antisemitic, even before, but now… Take it from me they are very zealous in their work.'

'I understand,' I replied, saddened that being a Jew here was not the simple state of affairs I had imagined. 'Mrs Huberman, I'm looking for the Jewish Aid Committee. I have no money. Perhaps they can find me somewhere to live for a few days.'

'Yes, I can tell you where it is: not far from here, in Rue Rosier. Otto knows it.'

It was a great help to have Otto as a guide through the narrow streets of this strange and wonderful city. On the way he said to me, 'Look, why don't you share with me, my room is just nearby? The way it works is that the Committee will give you some money every week for food and rent, along with a ration book. I know it's enough to cover the rent. That will help both of us out with my share, and we'll have some left over.' I readily agreed.

The Jewish Aid Committee occupied a large, official-looking room with several desks at which interviewing staff sat. I was given a number and sat down with a lot of other refugees many of whom were speaking French and Dutch to wait my turn. I did not have to wait long to be called forward. The interviewer asked me for my papers, and, although I produced my passport with the 'J' stamped on it, he was not satisfied but wanted to know my whole history. He asked about my parents, my brothers, even about Kristallnacht and everything I had seen on that night. He made sporadic notes as I talked until he seemed convinced that I was who I claimed to be and then issued me with a ration card.

Otto's room was on the top floor of a very old building and its main window led out on to a tiny balcony. 'If the Germans come,' he told me in an excited and conspiratorial tone, 'we can easily climb from the balcony onto the roof.'

The room was sparsely furnished with just two twin beds, a wardrobe, a couple of chairs, a plain table and a wash basin, ideal for two boys without much thought about tidying up. Outside the door was a shrivelled old plant in a pot. We solemnly agreed that in the happy event that one of us was entertaining a lady we would set this pot on its side. It was perhaps predictable that during my stay with Otto the pot remained stubbornly upright.

We went back to the restaurant, where Mrs Huberman told me, 'If you want to help out here in the kitchen you'll get a meal. Start tonight, but we're particularly busy on Saturday nights.'

And this is what I did, sometimes also working at lunchtime. 'Make sure you stay in the kitchen when we have customers,' Mrs Huberman had emphasised. 'To be seen will be very dangerous, for me as well as for you.'

I was glad of the food, and I often gave Mrs Huberman some of my ration cards, as these were scarce and useful to her to purchase supplies for the restaurant.

The kitchen area was large and busy. Otto and I washed and stacked plates, while Mrs Huberman supervised the preparation of the food by her cook and served in the restaurant. It was here that

I met Minna, her daughter, who also served in the restaurant and was an integral part of the family business. Minna was an attractive and vivacious girl with jet-black hair and a marvellous figure, but, in her mid-twenties, she was right out of our league. Not the least of her attractions was how capable she seemed. She was also flirtatious, though clearly not frivolous.

Otto adored Minna, and his eyes followed her everywhere. 'I'm sure I have a chance with her,' he used to say to me. But I couldn't imagine my innocent, studious new friend having any luck in that direction. He looked even younger – and was possibly even more immature – than I was.

'Otto,' I would sometimes say, 'she's just a friendly sort of girl, you know.' Minna was a natural flirt, one of those people who emphasise their remarks with a light touch to your arm, and whose eyes sparkle as if it were you making them sparkle. This was her charm. But Otto was not a complete fool and in sober moments conceded that perhaps her carefree laughter was occasionally aimed gently at our clumsy efforts to impress her.

Minna had a friend in the police who was sweet on her. I occasionally spied on him from behind the scenes when he came to the restaurant, which was always in the mornings, never at lunchtime. Naturally, he ate on a complimentary basis. He was a short, broad-shouldered man, and with his beret looked to me like a typical Frenchman. He would warn Minna of any imminent police searches for refugees and when such a day came we would close the restaurant.

A few days after I moved in with Otto we ventured into the red-light district of Pigalle and Montmartre. This soon became a habit during our leisure time, when we weren't helping out at the restaurant. We had started our trips dutifully enough as tourists in this great city; we visited the Eiffel Tower, strolled along the Champs-Élysées, then widened our sightseeing to include Montparnasse and the picturesque student quarter of St Michel, on the other side of the Seine. But it was the red-light district which drew us again and again and we soon gave up any pretence of wider cultural interest. Pigalle, with its prostitutes and nightclubs displaying photographs of topless dancers, and the raw sounds and smells of the area intoxicated us. We watched as uniformed doormen tempted the new tourists, German soldiers, with their poor German: *'Komm herein! Sehen sie die nackten Mädchen!* Come inside. See you the nude girls.' If they entered, those photographs of the dancers burst into life as we glimpsed the bare-breasted females on stage kicking out their legs to the accompaniment of the raucous music always heard in the narrow, thronging streets of Montmartre's sex market.

Very soon we fancied ourselves to be connoisseurs of the place. We suavely distinguished between such down-market places as the Cabaret Eve or Le Paradis, the haunts of the German soldiery, and the up-market Bal Tabarin and Moulin Rouge, with their gilt and velvet trappings and mainly French clientele. We only wished we had the money for any of these places, high or low, but the price of entry was a costly drink.Yet despite our obvious youth, we were routinely accosted by prostitutes on street corners, and were temporarily enveloped in the heady aroma of their cheap perfume. But always the price they sought was too high for us, so that it was all just a titillating but frustrating game.

Evenings at Chez Huberman were bustling occasions. Because I was confined to the kitchens I never once saw Mrs Huberman with her customers, but it was obvious that she was on familiar terms with them. 'This for Pierre! That for Madeleine!' she would call as she came through the kitchen doors with the orders, a spotless white apron round her wide waist.

There was indeed a Mr Huberman, who was a quiet, rather grey person compared with his vibrant wife and daughter. If you addressed him he peered at you over a pair of spectacles, his expression the same as the one he wore as he sat at his counting table methodically issuing bills or placing the takings in a solid metal box. Mr Huberman seemed altogether much older and I never made any real connection with him.

During family meals in the closed restaurant Mrs Huberman would chat intimately about her customers' families. Minna, under the wistful gaze of Otto, sometimes sang for us and we occasionally harmonised with her. 'I love Edith Piaf,' she would say. 'People think my voice is like hers. Do you think it is?' It was quite remarkably similar, strong, metallic and vibrant. There was one sentimental Piaf song she sang that especially entranced me. 'L'Accordéoniste' was about a street-corner prostitute who, after work, went to a dance hall, not to dance but to listen to her lover, who played a dance called a Java on his accordion. But the player went away to war and died. The girl is alone on the street corner:

La fille de joie est belle
Au coin de la rue là-bas
Elle a une clientèle
Qui lui remplit son bas
Quand son boulot s'achève
Elle s'en va à son tour
Chercher un peu de rêve
Dans un bal du faubourg
Son homme est un artiste

95

C'est un drol d'un petit gars
Un accordéoniste
Qui sais jouer la java.

At other times we would anxiously debate the political situation, which was, after all, our situation. 'Pétain said he will protect all French citizens,' Mrs Huberman told us one day, 'but we were born in Poland. Does that include us?' Nobody knew. 'Minna, you will be safe, you were born here,' she said. 'I want to stay here, this is my home,' Minna replied. But on another occasion Minna spoke of a friend who had some money in Switzerland. He had tried to enter Switzerland illegally, but the Swiss handed him over to the SS, and he had ended up in a concentration camp. Although he had taken on French nationality, he had been born in Poland. 'I know, I know,' said Mrs Huberman, 'perhaps your father and I are not safe here, perhaps I should sell this restaurant and get to the South, where it is safe.' All we could do was speculate.

I was far from home, and in this environment of Jewish family life my thoughts ceaselessly returned to my parents. But what could I do with such thoughts, which were a torment to me? I had written once to my parents when I arrived in Paris in December 1940, but I heard nothing from them and gave up writing.[1] My decision to write no more was made partly because to do so was to risk revealing to prying eyes where I was living.

Still, for the time being all we could do was lead our lives in as normal a way as possible and hope for the best. And nothing could keep Otto and me away from the red-light district. It was on one of our forays that I became intrigued by the activities of a certain Mediterranean-looking young man, smartly dressed in suit and tie, who would accompany German soldiers to the doors of cabarets and then return at once to the street. Otto was focused on the pictures of half-naked girls and I was glad of this, because I had no intention of sharing what had sprung into my mind. It was obvious to me that the man in the suit was making money. As he disappeared and returned to a cabaret with more soldiers, I watched and saw him scribble on a piece of paper, which he handed to the doorman, before disappearing back across the square.

That night, while Otto chatted on about dancers and prostitutes, I was elsewhere, and did not even consider including Otto in my plans. The cabaret man, with his dark looks, might conceivably have been a Jew, but there could be no doubt about Otto. His naivety was bad enough but his looks disqualified him entirely from the adventure I was planning. All fellowship with Otto counted for nothing. I well knew that my desire for adventure was connected to an urge to escape the whole Jewish world of Otto and the Hubermans. Even as I acknowledged this to myself I felt shame that my mind was working against my friends in this way, but I knew that to survive it was necessary to think like the Nazi conquerors among whom I lived, to remove myself as far as possible from the people they hated; in fact, to remove myself from myself.

The very next evening, while Otto was helping out at the restaurant, I travelled on the Métro to Pigalle among a crowd of eager-faced German soldiers. I emerged with them into the bright neon lights and crossed over the square to the cabarets, my eyes searching for the smartly dressed young man. Perhaps I'd find him at the Cabaret Eve, where I now listened to the doorman tempting the German soldiers. Some of them, already drunk, just laughed and moved on, but others entered. Yet I could not spot my man. Perhaps he was not working tonight. I was wondering what do next when suddenly he came into view, making his way towards Pigalle Métro station. I followed. When he got there I waited to see what he would do.

Soon enough the Métro disgorged another group of soldiers. My man approached one of them and I was close enough to hear him talking to his target in atrocious, accented German. How much better I would be at that task! I thought. I listened in fascination as he spoke to the soldier, while others now gathered around, attracted by his pitch. 'I will take you to special shows, private ones, very exclusive indeed, where you will see thirty-two positions of love-making,' he promised them. At this I momentarily forgot the reason I was there. *Thirty-two*? I thrashed around in my mind in wild speculation about this number. What could it mean? It was its exactitude which so perplexed me. Meanwhile my man had obviously scored another success because he led the group away and I waited anxiously for his return.

When he returned to his post at the Métro, I steeled myself and approached. I excused myself politely and spoke to him. 'Look, I'm a refugee from Metz. I'm penniless here in Paris. My German is very good, so I think I can be of some use to you. I've been watching you and understand how you make a living. To be frank, I need some money. My name is Robert.'

He looked me up and down and nodded, giving nothing away. At close quarters I could see that he was a sharp-featured fellow with sunken cheeks. 'Come with me,' he said; just three words, but perhaps the password to a new life. I felt light-headed as he led me to a nearby bistro. He ordered wine and, while I adjusted to the fact that this was really happening to me, he commenced negotiations. 'My name is Christos,' he began. 'I come from Greece. Introducing you to the clubs is worth a lot of money, you know – they give a percentage of their take to the middle man.'

'Well, as I said, I have no money, but how about me giving you a percentage of anything I make?' I was hardly able to believe that this was Freddie Knoller speaking, the innocent Viennese schoolboy. Yet Christos seemed to consider my suggestion seriously. He nodded again and, to my astonishment, our deal was struck.

We then got down to the details. 'I start work at seven in the evening. I usually go on till three in the morning,' said Christos. How would we collect our commission? And how would I take it to him? We sorted these matters out easily enough, but at the end Christos leant forward with a meaningful expression on his face and said, 'Just a little warning.' With his hard, experienced manner, he seemed much older than me, but it turned out that there were only two years between us. 'If you try to cheat me,' he went on, 'I have certain friends who will take care of things... You won't be seen in Pigalle after that, I can tell you.' I earnestly assured him he would never regret trusting me.

'Still,' he went on, 'if we become friends I won't mind you having some of the action. There are so many soldiers around here, I can't handle them all.' Despite his tough talk, I felt I could like Christos. More importantly, I sensed that I could trust him, but for now I just thanked him profusely for the chance he was giving me.

We drank some more, and the conversation came around to the question of accommodation. 'I'm sharing with another refugee,' I explained.

Christos thought for a moment, then said, 'Look, why don't you share with me? I've got a room around the corner from here, small, but fine for two. You'll have to pay half the rent, of course, once you start earning.' I accepted at once. Christos's place was nearby, on the top floor of a hotel in Rue des Martyrs and, once he had shown it to me, he gave me a spare key.

I went back to spend the last night in the room I shared with Otto, a new key in my pocket, a different future beckoning. I was much too excited to sleep and occasionally looked towards the shape of Otto in the bed beside me. He always worked in the restaurant at lunchtime, so that would be the ideal time to leave, I told myself, sensing the burden of being a Jew among Jews lifting from my shoulders. The next day I packed the few things I had and left, leaving only the spare key on the table, but no note.

So it was in this furtive manner that I abandoned my new friend and the kindly Hubermans, and separated myself from my Jewish identity. It would be the Nazis who would, in a few years' time, repatriate me to that identity. For now, I was about to enter the magical, privileged world of non-Jews.

Christos and I had agreed to meet again at Place Pigalle and he wasted no time when we did. After dropping off my suitcase in his room we were back on the street and heading for the clubs. I had initiated this new life, but I was dazed at how quickly it was taking shape.

Our first stop was the Le Paradis in Rue Fontaine. Christos introduced me to the doorman and then the manageress. My customers, she told me, would be noted under the name of Robert and I would receive five per cent of the money spent by these clients.

Next my new friend took me to a brothel, at 122 Rue de Provence, a narrow street lined with tall buildings. This was, I learnt, a famous venue. There was a large area where the girls were seated at the bar and at tables, drinking with German officers and civilians. These girls wore transparent blouses, some casually exposing their breasts and even their lower parts. Christos merely laughed as I reddened in embarrassment. 'If you want to do this work you'd better get used to seeing naked girls,' he said. I absorbed the lesson that it was one thing to indulge an adolescent fantasy, another to see the reality so casually, almost brutally displayed. I was introduced to Madame Jamet, the owner of the brothel. Naturally Christos did most of the talking, but, once I had got over the sight of the girls, I was so overwhelmed by the luxurious interior of number 122 that I could not help saying to Madame Jamet, 'What a beautiful place you have here!' I shook my head as I gazed around at the tall mirrors, which reflected the great, sparkling chandelier overhead.

She laughed graciously and said, 'Let me show you some of my rooms.' Upstairs she opened doors on to one wonder after another, for every room of pleasure was a bold, brash representation of a foreign country. There was the Spanish room and the Chinese room, and many others. I particularly remember the Arabian room. A baldachin of heavy gold drapes cascaded luxuriously around the large bed, the walls were frescoed with belly dancers; lights, encrusted with coloured glass, hung from a golden chandelier. Such gaudy magnificence dedicated solely to the pursuit of pleasure lifted me on to a plane of prospects as remote as the region it depicted. All I could do was click my tongue in amazement, while behind me Madame Jamet laughed in delight at my boy's appreciation of her establishment.

For all that I had abandoned the Jewish world, I only had to turn left out of Madame Jamet's and walk a little way along Rue de Provence before the street became Rue Richer, where Chez Huberman was. Yet that short journey seemed an ocean's width now.

Christos next introduced me to what he called a 'private house', this one in Rue Navarin, near Pigalle. Here, the madam explained, the client may watch two women performing sexually with each other and, for an extra sum, could enjoy himself with them after the show. Such shows were particularly expensive. 'Don't bring German civilians here,' Christos cautioned me. A 'private house' was a euphemism for an unregistered one, and a civilian might be a Gestapo man.

'You'll have to buy a suit and shirt and tie,' said Christos, scrutinising my workaday waterproof jacket and shabby trousers. 'You can't operate looking like that.' My new friend took me to a clothing store on Boulevard Montmartre. 'I'll lend you the money for one,' he said, 'but you'll need two. Buy the second as soon as you've earned yourself enough commission.'

Christos and the proprietor of the store clearly knew each other well. I noticed that my new friend did not use his ration card to pay for the suit but handed over cash, a black-market deal, which made the suit an expensive purchase. I looked at myself in the shop mirror, in a double-breasted navy-blue suit with a pinstripe. Yes, quite the operator, I thought. I liked the world I had landed in.

I lay awake that night, my head spinning. Next to me, in a similar single bed, with a similar rust-coloured bedspread, slept Christos. I marvelled at how different in every respect this room was from the one I had so recently shared with Otto – that poor attic dwelling, the walls stinking of moisture from a porous roof. And how untidy I and Otto had been there, with clothes left lying around and beds in disarray. It had been a luxury just to have a roof over our heads. We were just boys, used to being looked after by our mothers, and perhaps we had not tried to make a home in a place we might have to flee at any moment.

Christos's place was just another single room with twin beds, but the similarity ended there. The beds were properly made up. There was the small homeliness of the table cloth, with its pleasing blue-and-red check, and at the table a third chair set as if for any visitor who might appear. The water jug and the bowl stood on a chest of drawers. We got water from a sink in the corridor. On the wall was a large print of a pastoral scene at which I would often gaze. It looked seventeenth-century to me and showed a group of people picnicking in a meadow under a blue sky with wispy clouds. I admired the skill of the artist in rendering these cloud formations, but it was the depiction of an unperturbed and timeless scene of quiet enjoyment which most affected me, as if I might, just by focusing on it intently enough, manage to enter its timeless world.

Christos had rules. For a start, we could not leave without making the beds and, he informed me, 'We take it in turns here to clean and dust,' so alerting me to another of his regulations.

The attention Christos paid to the appearance of his room went beyond mere pride or the possession of a tidy nature. For the settled comfort of his room seemed to reflect, above all, his perfectly lawful presence in Paris.

I was rudderless, virtually friendless, and in constant danger of discovery, but I felt like a bird released from its cage. I had found my ingenuity and independent spirit. The boy I was, who had gone nowhere and done nothing without his parents, had carved out for himself this undreamt of new adventure. I should have been a college boy; instead I was a going to be a sort of pimp. Of course, apart from the fumbling experience with our maid and the disastrous one with the prostitute in Antwerp, I had enjoyed little sexual adventure. But real sexual experience, I was sure, could only be just around the corner. Now that I wore a suit it was time to abandon my knapsack, and it felt like a break with my childhood when I dumped it and bought a small suitcase in its place.

And so it was, along with Christos, that I took up my post for the first time outside Pigalle Métro station. As neon asserted itself against the failing light of day I waited for the soldiers, my first soldiers, to appear. Soon came the clang of boots on the iron-lipped steps. I felt strangely unafraid at this sound and watched the soldiers as they rose in a mass to street level. The greenish-grey of the Wehrmacht mingled with the grey of the Luftwaffe, whose orange collar tabs were a distinctive feature. The officers, with their peaked caps, shiny buttons and polished leather shoes gave an impression of real elegance in wartime Paris. I myself was sober, almost drab, in my plain suit and tie. Christos, who after all had introduced me to this way of life, would always have first choice. I waited for him to make a successful approach before I moved in.

My remarkable asset was my perfect German. As I approached my first target the patter came to me with suave assurance, as if I had been performing this role all my life.

'*Guten Abend, Meine Herren.*'

They paused, and looked me over, seeing a smiling, fair-haired and clean-cut young man. In perfect German I offered my services as a guide to the nightlife of Paris. 'Gentlemen, I will lead you to such pleasures as you have only imagined. I will take you to shows where nude girls will dance for you. I will find you the most passionate girls ever. I will show you the Paris of your dreams.'

'How come you speak such good German?' the soldiers asked me.

The lie came smoothly to my lips. 'I come from Alsace, where everybody speaks German. My own father is German, my mother French. I went to school in Vienna. And my name is Robert.' One of the reasons I was so plausible is that I half believed my own story. Until that moment my false identity had been the last resort of a fugitive. Now it was a means to an end, a tool for making a living under the very nose of the enemy.

The soldiers laughed in surprised delight at coming across a loyal, welcoming friend in the land they had conquered, one who spoke like them, looked like them and was so at ease with them. Besides, with the promises I had made them of so many delights, they wanted to like me. The ease with which I took the Germans in only fortified my belief in my new identity. The Germans were the mirror in which I saw myself. If they believed in me, I believed in me. By this psychological sleight of hand I became an Alsatian.

'Follow me, gentlemen,' I said. And they did follow me, as would hundreds of other soldiers for the next two years.

Their eyes would widen at the door of the Cabaret Eve as they gazed at its salacious, tinted photographs of dancing girls. Sometimes they got no further than here, and might reward me with a handful of francs. The commissionaire would smile at the soldiers entering his establishment and mark me down for a commission. But Cabaret Eve was not my preferred destination for the soldiers. I wanted to manoeuvre them farther along, to Le Paradis, where my commission was higher than in most other places. I moved on with those I had retained, along the narrow, cobbled Rue Pigalle towards Rue Fontaine. There was temptation everywhere. Almost every doorway belonged to a nightclub, all displaying similar photographs, while all along the way ladies of the night either called out or simply accosted us. But, despite these distractions, I usually succeeded in getting my group to Rue Fontaine, at the bottom of Rue Pigalle, where frenzied music spilled out from Le Paradis. The doorman permitted my soldiers a tantalising view of a chorus line of dancing girls performing on stage. Le Paradis was not a high-class place but a spot for foreign visitors. As we entered, my clients were immediately surrounded by the girls and led to tables near the stage. I gave a slip of paper with my name on it to the commissionaire. On it he marked down the number of soldiers I had brought. Then he noted the table number where they were sitting, usually already drinking beer, while the girls who had joined them took professional sips at their champagne cocktails. Sometimes I would get another gift of francs from the soldiers, a smile of gratitude, a slap on the back, and be told what a fine fellow I was.

After I had lived with Christos for long enough to get myself on my feet financially, I moved into my own room in the Hôtel du Collège Rollin, in Rue de Douai. This was one of the many small hotels in Pigalle where prostitutes took their clients, but to me it was home, and following Christos's example, I began to take a pride in the appearance of my room. Perhaps I did so because I was beginning to feel established, or perhaps because I was beginning to feel myself a man, with the manly responsibility of making my own way in life. Perhaps, too, because of my now complete sense of oneness with my assumed identity.

Every night it was the same routine with the soldiers. But one particular evening was quite different from any other. For some reason I was at my post earlier than usual, not much later than seven in the evening. Normally I did not arrive until eight o' clock, because it was rare to see the soldiers about in Pigalle before then. On this evening it was a single soldier who emerged from the Métro. It was normal in my world to approach a lone soldier, but you never knew whether he might be with others. But this soldier seemed to me to have a solitary air about him. He gazed around without appearing to take in much of his surroundings. He looked like a candidate for Le Paradis, so I went up to him.

'Cabaret? Nude girls?' I propositioned. After the usual questions about my perfect German we started walking along Rue Pigalle. 'I am glad to be in a civilised country like France, I can tell you,' he remarked. 'Do you want to join me for a drink?'

As it was so early, I agreed. Sometimes the soldiers encouraged me to stay with them at Le Paradis or whichever club I took them to, but I never stayed unless invited. And whenever I did I would take my leave as soon as politeness permitted, thinking of all the business outside that I might be missing. But now, with about an hour before the military arrived in number, the invitation was easy enough to accept.

When we arrived at Le Paradis the manageress beckoned to a table near the stage. 'No, no,' said the soldier to me, 'I don't want that, too noisy, too bright. Farther back, please.' I explained this to the manageress. We sat down and he introduced himself to me. 'Helmut's my name,' he said, extending his hand.

'Robert,' I replied.

The champagne arrived, and though he kept swallowing one glass after another, this did not seem to make my new friend any happier. He began talking to me, not in the usual way of most of the soldiers, but as if he really needed someone to whom he could unburden himself. 'I am from a little place near Munich. I am twenty-eight. I got married four years ago.' He paused, on his face the sad and reflective look of a man who has learnt some hard lessons. 'Went in the army, then my wife writes to me, I get the letter out there... Do you know where I've been? The Russian Front ... nobody wants to go there. We are dying like flies, it's terrible. And the cold, that damned, freezing cold. My wife sends me a letter, she wants a divorce... She's met someone else... Can you believe that?'

Helmut drained the bottle and ordered another. He might have been a German, but I was feeling sorry for him. His descriptions of the hardships on the Russian Front were vivid and terrible and they moved me even though I could not help but remain aware of the commission the bottles he ordered would bring me.

'You know what happened out there, in Russia?' He paused, looking at me intently, as if perhaps I really might know. 'My best friend, killed.'

He had tears in his eyes. He shook his head. '*Verdammter Krieg… Verdammter Krieg*. Damned war,' he kept saying. I nodded along with him; I had my own reasons for cursing this war, but they were reasons I could not share with Helmut.

Helmut slumped forward across the table. I had spent an unusual hour or so with him, but it was time for me to leave. Other potential clients would be making their way to the tawdry glitter of Pigalle.

On 14 May 1941, within a few months of my leaving Chez Huberman, the infamous *rafles* of Paris began. The streets were suddenly full of gendarmes. 'They're rounding up Jews,' said Christos. I watched helplessly from the sidelines as these French policemen entered buildings and came out with their captives, whose only crime was their Jewishness. Often it was whole families they took, pushing them roughly into the waiting police vehicles, indifferent to their age, sex or state of health.

Mrs Huberman had been right about the gendarmes; their zeal appalled me. I saw not a single SS man or Gestapo officer in sight. The German persecution of the Jews had driven me from Austria, then Belgium and now here in France it was something even worse: the willingness of a defeated nation to do the dirty work of their so-called enemy.

I had known about the collaboration for some time, but now I was seeing it in its full viciousness, and it was a bitter pill to swallow. Where now was the ringing French motto *Liberté, Égalité, Fraternité*? Those whose motto it was had been shown to be quite unworthy of its bold sentiment.

When I witnessed these scenes I reproached myself that I was a Jew who had abandoned his own people. It was impossible not to identify with other Jews, nor to keep from my mind the thought that any of them might have been one of my own family, whom I thought about daily.

One day Christos and I were sitting in our favourite bistro, in Rue des Martyrs. I had drunk a lot of wine and felt in a confiding mood. The restaurant was almost empty. 'Why are you so miserable today?' Christos asked. My relationship with him had long ceased to be merely a business one. We were friends, but although I trusted him completely, I could not at first tell him what was troubling me. In his gentle way he persisted. 'I know am your friend, your true friend. Let me help you.'

His words so touched me that tears sprang to my eyes. 'Christos,' I said, 'thank you for being my friend.' The urge to reveal the truth about myself was beginning to overwhelm any thought of self-preservation. I had seen enough of Jews being rounded up on the streets. I had lived long enough in hiding, not just from the Germans, but from myself. I decided to make my confession. 'I will tell you why I am crying and so unhappy. I know I am putting my life in your hands by telling you this. The truth is that I am a Jew from Vienna, a refugee from Hitler and my real name is Freddie Knoller.'

I waited for Christos's reaction. He sat back in his seat, raised his eyebrows and nodded slowly. 'I just never thought of that,' he murmured, almost to himself, then immediately asked in alarm, 'What papers do you have?' I told him about my German passport with the 'J' stamped on it. Next I produced my fake *Sauveteur Médaillé* card. Christos exploded when he saw this, no doubt as angry with himself as with me for not checking up on my identification papers in the first place. 'What do you think you are doing,' he railed at me, 'going up to the *Boches* with a tinpot forgery like this? Are you mad?' He at once answered his own question. 'You must be. Do you want to rot in some jail? If the French police get a look at these they'll hand you over to the Gestapo, I suppose you know that. And what do you think will happen to me, as your associate? I'll come in for some tough questioning, too. And whatever they decide to do with me, I won't be able to work again, that's for sure.' He sighed, his anger soon dissolving, as was his way. 'I suppose you have guts at least, even if no brains.' He would try to sort something out, he said.

And so my friend Christos adjusted to the fact that I was not Robert, who spoke German because he was from Metz, but a Jew called Freddie, a refugee from Vienna. I never had cause to regret confiding in Christos.

On to the scene came a friend of Christos, who introduced himself as Pierre Marcello, a sharply dressed, tall, rakish, good-looking young Corsican with a very distinctive hairstyle, a high-swept, ostentatious plume. Right from the start he and I liked each other. Pierre had a sideline – one of many, I was to learn – in false papers. 'This will be expensive,' he said, 'very expensive.'

'How much?' I asked. Pierre's price was very high.

'You'll have to give me most of it now, and the rest you can pay back in instalments. Christos says you can be trusted.'

'Yes, you can trust me.' Another thought then occurred to me. 'I was just thinking about getting a ration card, now that I am a French citizen.' The period at Chez Huberman, when I had been able to get a card from the Jewish Aid Committee, had been a short one: soon after this refugees were unable to obtain a card. Or perhaps one was only given to a refugee on a first application, I cannot be sure. In fact, since Mrs Huberman had laughed at my old false papers I had never tried to present them to obtain a ration card.

'The documents I'm going to get you will get past any inspection,' Pierre assured me.

I had yet another thought. 'Maybe, but these papers say I am from Alsace. What if…?'

Pierre knew what I was afraid of. 'Look, I can assure you, there is no communication between the French authorities here and Alsace. Don't you see? Alsace is now a part of Germany.' I nodded. I knew this, but I sought reassurance.

It was obvious to me that Pierre had genuine sympathy for me in my predicament. We became good friends. He soon supplied me with a French identity card. It looked very convincing to me. I was sure that with this document I was a much more believable 'Robert Metzner, born in Metz'. This Alsatian origin, as I had already proved with the soldiers, lent plausibility to my German accent. Another factor was that there were quite a number of Alsatian refugees in Paris, so there was nothing in my assumed origin to arouse suspicion.

My first visit to the Mairie to obtain a ration card was an ordeal. It was the first time I presented my new false papers. Would they hold up under an official inspection? Never mind all Pierre's suave assurances. You just never knew. In the event they passed muster and I was given a card. Now I could obtain rations again.

111

If, in my very first approach to the German military in Pigalle, I had half believed my own story, now these splendid false papers made me feel as if I were truly a different person. Their skilful approximation of authenticity seemed to ratify my story: I was a Frenchman from Alsace, I had been born in Metz. I was not Freddie Knoller but Robert Metzner. I felt safe.

And so my life on the streets continued and I could have been happy in this work for the rest of the war, but it was not to be.

As I refined my procurer's skills, my preferred quarry soon became the German officer class, who could afford the services of Madame Jamet's exclusive establishment in Rue de Provence. It needed the same perseverance I exercised with the common soldiery to steer them through the temptations along the way. The beckoning prostitutes who lined the streets, their legs dyed a shade of tan in the wartime absence of silk stockings, all knew me, and they begged me to introduce them to my German friends, offering me a percentage. 'Maybe later,' I responded to them in their patois, with an easy smile, but I guarded my investment in the German officers jealously. To them, in German, I said, 'These girls are not clean.' How duplicitous I had become. But my words usually did the trick, until the next corner, where similar offers were made. I then had to negotiate the officers past the Bal Tabarin, that superior venue where, crucially, no commissions were on offer.

Finally we would arrive at 122 Rue de Provence. It was at this point that my party normally seemed to have doubts about my judgement. This was understandable, because the great oak door and shiny, small brass plaque on the wall with the plain name Madame Jamet gave a very sedate impression after the garish offerings of Pigalle. 'Just trust me,' I would urge my hesitant group.

Top: My family, 1936. (From left to right) Me – Fredy – aged 15; my mother, Marja; Otto, aged 23; my father, David; Eric, aged 17.

Below: The courtyard of our apartment block at Untere Augartenstrasse 32. Our neighbour, Mr Epstein, died here on Kristallnacht, when the Brownshirts hurled him from his apartment window.

Above: The Knoller trio, 1936: me with cello, Eric with violin, and Otto at the piano. Mama, Papa and our dear neighbour, Fraulein Schiff (far right) were always our admiring audience.

Right: Wizo programme dated 14 December 1935. The appearance of Die Brüder Knoller is underlined.

Empfangsabend der Wizo II

Programm

zu der am Samstag, den 14. Dezember 1935 Wien, I. Schottenring 25, präzise 8 Uhr stattfindenden

AKADEMIE

1. Begrüßung
2. Herr Oberkantor Rottenberg
3. Trio der Brüder Knoller
   Klavier, Geige, Cello
4. Herr Halpern, Tenor
5. Frl. Lisl Weinberger, Tanzsoubrette
6. Herr Polnau, aus der Reinhardtbühne

PAUSE

7. Frl. Rosl Safier, Vortrag und Chansons
8. Herr Ernst Drimmer,
   Jazzsänger und Stepptänzer
9. Josef Kamen, Willner-Truppe

Technische und musikalische Begleitung Otto Knoller.

Top left: My father sent this postcard to Eric in the USA c. 1940. Note the letters 'Isr', the shortened form of 'Israel', which all Jewish males were obliged to add to their name under Nazi racial laws. The equivalent form for Jewish females was 'Sarah'.

Top right: My family attended the Polnische Tempel, which was burned to the ground during Kristallnacht, 9 November 1938.

Below: The school I attended from the age of twelve.

Top: Nazi party publicity on a Viennese tram for the planned plebiscite of 10 April 1938, which did not take place because of the Anschluss of 11 March 1938.

Below left: Placard barring Jews from a park: 'We don't want to see Jews; Jews are our misfortune'.

Below right: Poster for an antisemitic exhibition at the Northwest Railway station hall in Vienna. The caption reads: 'The Eternal Jew'

The Drancy transit camp. Léo Bretholz can be seen in the right angle of the building, beret, scarf and white object under his right arm. We were not at Drancy at the same time.

Top left: Yvonne, the girl I met in Paris two weeks after my liberation from Belsen, April 1945. She was also a survivor of Auschwitz.

Top right: Dr Bennetin (*standing next to me*), with whose kindly family I recuperated in Salornay-sur-Guy in Loire, May 1945.

Below left: Dr Bennetin took this photograph of me in my concentration camp clothing.

Below right: The chemist's daughter, Janine, with whom I flirted in Salornay.

Top: Me (*left*) with my cousin Rosi and her husband Max Schäechter, after the war.

Below left: Myself and Leo Bretholz collecting our US visas from the consulate in Bordeaux, 1946.

Below right: I met Pierre Heimrath, my companion from Drancy to the Death March, in Marseilles after the war.

Freda and I married in Baltimore on 31 December 1950.

Inset: I met the Queen at the opening of the Holocaust Exhibition at the Imperial War Museum, 2000.

I would rap on the door, and a concealed square panel in the centre would slid back. The eyes of Madame Jamet looked out. *'Robert! Entrez! Entrez!'* The solid door opened at once. And then, from behind me, came the gasps of surprise and pleasure. *'Schöne Mädchen! Sehr schön!'* Straight ahead, perched by a bar, were a dozen or so of the beautiful young women, who, clad as revealingly as always, smiled at the new arrivals.

Madame Jamet offered her new arrivals cognac and champagne. The officers in their stiff grey uniforms were ushered to one of the low round tables and cocooned in the luxurious armchairs. The girls did not pester the men; they waited to be chosen. The men gave themselves up to the ambience of the salon, while Madame Jamet, a flame-haired woman always in long, decorous skirts, and striking-looking even in her forties, fussed over her new clients. She joked and flirted with them, teasing her curls, which set her many bracelets in tinkling motion.

Apart from the beauty of her girls, there was always something for the eye to dwell on at Madame Jamet's. Here and there were great vases of flowers. Paintings of Folies Bergère-style chorus girls dotted the walls. The vast mirror softly amplified the scene. The baroque gilded ceiling would not have disgraced a Venetian palace. In a corner a gramophone crooned love songs.

Here, too, I was sometimes invited to join my group. I sat, smiled, and drank dutifully, but never for long. We toasted our new-found friendship and though I did not even enjoy the taste of champagne, it was my percentage I always had in mind as we drank to German victories. My officers liked to boast of their campaigns, declaring that only Britain resisted and she could not hold out for long. When the officers made their selection of the girls it was time for me to depart, sometimes with a wad of francs.

'Robert you are a great guy, a true friend,' they said.

In May 1942 I began to see for the first time in my life people wearing the yellow star of Jewish identity. These were French Jews, of course, as no illegal refugee would ever come forward for registration. Further raids followed, on a larger scale: there was the '*Grand Rafle*' of Jews on 16–17 July 1942, when I saw the streets flooded with gendarmes arresting those with the yellow star, their French countrymen, now so easily identifiable. But I was not to know the destination or fate of these herded Jews, and others before them, until I became one of their number a year later.

Around this time I was leading a group of officers along Pigalle to Rue de Provence when two young men walked towards us wearing the yellow star. As soon as they saw us they crossed to the other side of the street. I felt this as a terrible rebuke. I was once again seized by that urge to declare myself, to live again as a Jew, to be Freddie Knoller once more, not this person sedulously courting the enemy for money. As my party approached Madame Jamet's I understood how utterly alone I really was. In Paris, I was now cut off from my Jewishness. In opting for my life with Christos I did not visit the Hubermans. At first this may have been my uneasy feelings over the way in which I had parted from them and from Otto, but with the coming of the rafles it would have been dangerous to go into the Jewish quarter anyway.

One day I was caught up in a mass arrest. Pigalle Métro station was surrounded by German soldiers and French gendarmes. I was held there with other detainees for many hours.

An officer, hearing my German accent, questioned me. 'You are German?'

'No, from Alsace,' I said, and once again, because in my own mind I believed my story, I acted with brash assurance.

He examined my papers and nodded. 'What do you do?'

I explained.

'That's what you are then,' he said with mild contempt, 'a *Schlepper*.' This term, literally meaning to move in a dragging manner, was used to denote a low-class guide such as me. But such an insult did not trouble me. Indeed, I was pleased to be so classified.

My picaresque life in the streets of Paris carried on. I enjoyed sexual adventures that would never have been mine at home. I was out of my depth, of course, and trouble often followed. I had casual relationships with some of the waitresses and dancers. I suppose my association with Christos and Pierre leant me a certain glamour, but I was still a boy in a man's world.

Two romantic adventures I remember well, with Yvette and Monique. Yvette was a dancer at the Moulin Rouge, which was not a place to which I escorted any soldiers because, like the Bal Tabarin, there was no commission on offer in such a high-class place. I first met her at a bistro in Rue Lepic, where Christos and I often ate. Yvette was a flirt, and I responded.

'She has a boyfriend from Corsica, which means he's tough,' Christos warned me, 'so I'd keep well away if I were you.' But I took no notice because I found Yvette very appealing, with her long, blonde hair, blue eyes, good figure, and particularly her well-developed bust. She was older than me, but looked young. We started meeting for drinks, and one day Yvette suggested we should go dancing at the fashionable Chez Ledoyen, an expensive venue standing alone in the park off the Champs-Élysées. In the summer, you could eat and drink outside in the attractive garden. The main draw at the time was the swing band of Alex Combell.

Yvette offered to pay for the drinks. She was a generous girl, who knew I did not have a lot of money. Of course, she didn't know that out of my earnings I was still paying Pierre back for my expensive papers and Christos for my black-market suit. On top of that, the second suit I had bought had made a large hole in my earnings. 'But we have to do something about your appearance before we go to Chez Ledoyen,' concluded Yvette

I knew what she was getting at. In Paris at that time the young all wanted to be a *Zazou*. You saw the *Zazous* everywhere. This youth cult involved a special style of dress – for males it was drainpipe trousers and a large, chunky-shouldered jacket, that reached to the thigh. You also had to be sure that your shoes were unpolished. Yvette could afford the female attire of short, pleated skirt, high-heel shoes of wood and jacket with padded shoulders, but the most I could do for myself was to buy a cheap pair of dark glasses, another essential item of clothing for a *Zazou*. Leaving my shoes unpolished was easy enough.

I never got beyond flirting with Yvette. One day I was sitting in the bistro in Rue des Martyrs having a drink and waiting for Christos or Pierre when a mean-looking character came up to me. He did not introduce himself but said straight away in an aggressive manner, 'You, you're going out with my girlfriend.'

'What do you mean?' I replied, all innocence. From his appearance it was obvious that this was the Corsican Christos had warned me about.

'I'm talking about Yvette, and you have been going out with her.'

'What do you mean, "going out with her"? Look, I work in Montmartre and I go to all the cabarets and know a lot of girls, but I am not taking any girl out. I wouldn't go out with someone else's girlfriend.'

'Just stay away from her, that's all,' he said.

'Don't say I didn't tell you,' Christos said later as we sat in our bistro.

'OK, OK,' I replied, 'anyway, nothing much happened between us, in fact, nothing at all.'

'You were lucky. Now look,' said my good friend, 'let's go and hear the Hot Club de Paris.' Christos had no interest in dancing, but he loved swing music. I was very touched by his generosity when he slapped a ticket in my hand a few days later. 'On me,' he said.

And so, sitting with Christos in a crowded venue at the impressive Salle Gaveau concert hall, I heard the great jazz violinist Stéphane Grappelli, accompanied by Django Reinhardt, who played his guitar as if the two missing fingers of his left hand were no handicap at all. There were many small, inexpensive clubs in the Latin Quarter and I would often go on my own, or perhaps with some dancer I had met, to hear the fine swing music of the time.

Yvette's successor was Monique. Every working evening I would go alone or with Christos to collect our commission. Monique worked as a singer in two or three clubs, including Le Paradis. I would often see her perched on a stool at the bar at one or other of these clubs, a post-performance drink in her hand. I casually flirted with her because I can never resist flirting with women, but she was a lovely girl, blonde like Monique, though with her hair piled up on her head in a sophisticated manner. Everyone in Pigalle knew me, so Monique and I always said hello. One night I plucked up my courage to ask her out for dinner, and to my surprise and delight she accepted.

The next evening we were sitting at the bistro in Rue des Martyrs, whose owner, Pierrot, knew me well. Monique drank rosé and I my favourite, a *pastis*. I had chosen my moment well. Monique had a tale of woe to tell, all about her boyfriend. 'He's an actor. Well, he's been two-timing me. I should have known better after the first lie.'

'What was that?' I asked.

'He talked about marriage to me, then I found out he was already married.'

So, a lover and a wife – all very involved. 'We are both musicians, sensitive people, so we can get on well. I like you, Monique'

'Are you a musician, Robert?'

'Well, I play the cello, but I don't get much chance these days.'

'I didn't know that.'

It was that sort of conversation. She was depressed and I was playing the role of consoling friend to the hilt.

Monique said it was time for her to be going home, and indeed it was late. The clubs were closed and the streets quiet. 'Look, I can walk you home,' I suggested, and she agreed.

She lived not far away, in Rue du Faubourg Montmartre. When we got there she invited me inside for a coffee. It was a proper apartment, with a bathroom, not a single room like mine.

Our affair began on that very first night. I will always remember how lovely Monique looked when she released her hair from its prison of skilfully arranged combs. It was almost a shock to see how long it was as it cascaded over her shoulders.

Even at such moments I was on guard. I always made sure the lights were out and that I had a condom with me. The condom was only partly for the usual reasons. Like the darkened room, it served to hide my circumcision, evidence of a custom which was rarely practised outside Jewish circles in those days. Even in one of the many *pissotières* Paris had at that time I was careful about showing myself, and always glad if the place was empty.

I started to listen to Monique practising in the afternoons,

118

accompanying herself on the piano at Le Paradis. Her voice had an extraordinary range and I can still hear her singing the big hit of the day, 'J'attendrai'. She seemed to welcome my company and enjoyed my skill in harmonising the melodies. 'I can tell you are a musician, Robert!' she would exclaim.

The affair was very short-lived. I soon sensed Monique cooling, her smiles more automatic, her expression absent. 'Don't come home with me tonight, Robert,' she finally said while we were having lunch one day in Rue des Martyrs.

'Why not?'

'I have this job at the German Officers' Club in Versailles. The money there is very good. So it's better if...'

'I don't understand. We can meet afterwards, or tomorrow.'

'It won't be easy.'

'How did you get this job?' I asked, suspicion forming in my mind.

'Well, I met this German officer and he invited me to sing there.'

'I see, it's like that.'

'It's not like that.'

'Well, you couldn't have just met him and suddenly he's asking you to sing there.'

'All right. I have seen him a few times, he's a very nice person.'

The vision of this officer rose before my eyes. He was clearly the natural successor to the actor. In my mind they were one person, a suave, worldly, older man, with means to impress someone like Monique. In short, this amalgam possessed all the qualities I did not. I was seeing her now with this German, who no doubt had already bought her gifts of flowers and then probably stockings and jewellery. That was the usual progression. It was all so clear to me, and I felt a fool to have been under the illusion that I could be anything more than an interlude for the Moniques of this world.

'So that's it then, it's over between us,' I said. 'You have bigger fish to fry.'

'Don't be angry, Robert, we've had a good time, we can still be friends, you know.'

I never knew where Monique was from, whether she was from Paris or somewhere else in France, but I never saw her again. She disappeared from the scene entirely. I never found out what became of her.

I tried to console myself. I was at least an accepted part of the local nightlife, greeted cordially wherever I went, in brothels, clubs and bars. I was offered sex by some of the girls from Rue Pigalle but was never tempted, thinking of the sheer number of men – and particularly *Boches* – that they must have got through in a single day.

I always met Pierre and Christos at the bistro in the Rue des Martyrs. Pierre was a real pimp with quite a stable of prostitutes. He hated the *Boches*, he regularly declared at our bistro evenings. 'I'll take their money, no trouble, but collaborate with them?' He made an expression of disgust. This loathing of the Germans made him a particular favourite of mine.

One evening Pierre leant forward confidentially across the table. 'I have some very good contacts in the Resistance,' he said in a low voice. We, he intimated, should find out as much as possible from our clients: where they were stationed, the name of their unit, its strength, and any other information which might interest his 'friends'. I did my best to oblige, thinking back to the odd titbits I had picked up from officers I had taken to Madame Jamet's.

One day, after I had approached two German officers at Pigalle

Métro station, they invited me to have a drink with them. We ended up staying together the whole night, going from one nightspot to another, but naturally only to places where I had commission arrangements. The two officers drank a lot and after a while they became quite talkative. They were in charge of a unit just outside Versailles, they told me, specialising in finding 'terrorists and communists'. They told me they were looking in a small town near Versailles for a communist cell which was sabotaging German trucks and cars by slashing their tyres. They confided in me not only because they were drunk, but also because of my story about coming from Alsace and my declaration that I was a loyal German, delighted that Alsace was once again part of Greater Germany.

The next day I rushed to meet my friend Pierre, bursting with the news of my meeting with the officers, and gave him as much detail as I had gleaned. 'This is good, very good,' he said. 'Look, there is someone I want you to meet, one of my friends. Come to the bistro this evening.'

'Tell André what you told me,' said Pierre that evening. The man sitting with us was of small build, with a trim moustache, wearing a suit and glasses – a picture of unobtrusive, middle-aged neatness. But when I began to talk to André I became aware of a steely determination in him which at once commanded my attention. He listened intently, and never raised his voice or betrayed any excitement as he interjected with many questions. After this he began asking me about myself. He seemed thoroughly well prepared, working through a list of questions he had probably asked many times before. He wanted to know about my background in Vienna, my time in Belgium, the names of my aunt and uncle in Gaillac; he even wanted to know if I was circumcised. He asked me about my political views and I told him that I was a

121

member of the Socialist High School Students movement in Vienna and that I was and would always be a socialist. I couldn't answer all the questions he asked me about the officers, but he urged me to continue to keep my ear to the ground. 'Every small detail could be important to France,' he stressed. I smiled when he congratulated me. He instructed me to tell Pierre anything I heard. 'The Resistance will be grateful to you,' he concluded, and I felt exilarated.

One night I was, as usual, at Pigalle station when a civilian approached me. 'Can you direct me to Rue Victor Massé?' he asked. I realised he was German and became cautious, because although he did not wear the leather coat of the Gestapo, he still might have been one of them. I knew that there were many bars frequented by homosexuals in Rue Victor Massé, but I did not make any connection to his query.

As soon as I spoke in German he smiled. 'Oh, you speak German! Come on, let's have a drink together.' He seemed a very mild, pleasant fellow, so I gladly accompanied him to one of my haunts, where he ordered champagne.

'My name is Hans Kessler,' he began, 'I am a buyer for our army over here, for all sorts of things they might need. I find these things. There are deals to be had out there, if you know where to look. I will look to the black market if I have to.' My ears pricked up. This was Pierre Marcello's territory.

'Tell me about your background,' he asked, and I told him my story about Alsace and my life in Metz.

Hans seemed to have a lot of money. His mood became expansive with the champagne, and he ordered more. I was flattered that he seemed to prefer talking to me than paying attention to the hostesses or the floor show. After several hours he said, 'Look, Robert, it's closing here, but why don't you come with me to my hotel? We'll have another drink there. It's not very far.'

I happily agreed to this. I was enjoying spending time with Hans. He was such a gentle fellow, who did not boast about German greatness, and, besides, I had earned good commission from the amount of champagne he had drunk.

On the way back to his hotel he spoke, a little drunkenly, of his feelings about this war. 'Between you and me, I hate this damned war. So many fine young men dying.' He shook his head sadly. 'At the moment,' he said, changing the subject, 'I am looking for aluminium buckets for the army. That's what I am searching for, buckets. I need five thousand of them.'

'I'll see what I can do, I have contacts here who may be able to help.' There was commission in this for me if Pierre was interested in the deal.

Hans ordered champagne to be brought to his room. I declined more than a few sips, and he talked on. Then he put his arm around me. At first I thought this was just a comradely gesture brought on by drink, but when his other hand came to rest on my knee I realised that this was not the case. I drew back at once. Look,' said Hans softly, 'the truth is that I am not interested in women. I prefer men. You might enjoy this with me, you know.'

'Thank you very much,' I said stiffly, 'but I'm going now.'

I have to say that Hans was a gentleman about this rejection. 'I'm sorry,' he said, 'in my country under the Nazis, homosexuality is a serious offence, so I have to be very careful with whom I associate… That place in Rue Victor Massé, a friend told me about it. Won't you at least be my interpreter there? I respect your feelings and I won't approach you again in this way. Will you agree to this?'

123

I could tell that Hans was being sincere. He was so different in character to the run of German soldiery I dealt with in Pigalle, but the incident reminded me painfully that, despite my swaggering act of sophistication around Pigalle, I remained a naive boy who understood little of the world.

The next evening I took Hans to the club, where I took the owner aside. 'I am only an interpreter,' I explained. Hans, I told him, was a good man and, besides, seemed to have plenty of money. I called to Hans to join us and introduced him to the owner, who led us up to the first-floor apartment and acquainted Hans with two good-looking young men. One of them spoke some German, so I was no longer needed. Hans gave me a generous wad of notes, and I thanked him, adding, 'I'll be coming back to you about those buckets.' We made an arrangement to meet again.

Christos and Pierre were extremely interested in the subject of the buckets. 'I'll find them,' said Pierre, no problem. I'll give you a sample, and the price.' He assured me I would get a cut of the proceeds.

Aluminium bucket in hand, I met Hans again. He seemed more than pleased with it. We agreed a price and he gave me an official-looking order form with an address. Delivery was to be within two weeks. We had a drink in a bar, where Hans told me how grateful he was that I had been able to make the contact with the two nice young men and presented me with an envelope in recognition of my help. He then thanked me in his courteous way for my friendship, and that was the last time I ever saw Hans. The transaction went ahead, and I got my commission from Pierre.

The end of my Paris adventure came suddenly. One evening not long after I last saw Hans, I was negotiating as usual with the German soldiers when two civilians in long black leather coats, obviously Gestapo men, approached me. I froze. They demanded in French to see my papers. I had the presence of mind to reply in German.

'I see you are from Alsace, Herr Metzner,' one of them remarked, relaxing slightly. 'Your German is good.'

'Yes.'

'What are you doing here, talking to German soldiers?'

My heart beat furiously as I tried to make my answer seem casual. 'Oh, I'm a guide really. I show the soldiers around, the interesting sites, take them to some of the clubs... They can see the shows, the cabaret, things like that, no harm done. I speak German, so, you know, it's easy for me to get along with them.'

Both men nodded, but one said, 'You must come with us, Herr Metzner.'

They escorted me to a car and drove away. I gazed blankly out of the window on to the glittering Paris scene, wondering if I would ever be part of it again.

Gestapo headquarters was in an elegant building opposite the Opéra. The Gestapo men led me through a great arched entrance door beneath a huge swastika flag and a large sign reading 'Kommandantur' and into a nightmarishly echoing atrium with a central reception desk. I felt as insignificant as an insect in all these vast spaces. Brisk Nazi salutes exchanged with the official at the desk, the men accompanied me up a wide flight of stairs and into a sparsely furnished office.

There was a portrait of Hitler on the wall and the black, red and white of the swastika flag. But my eyes were drawn to the desk, because set on it, like some ornament, was a plaster-cast human skull and, next to this, a sheet of paper bearing a few large, clumsily reproduced Hebrew characters.

One of the Gestapo men left. The other sat behind the desk and indicated the chair on the other side. He studied me at length before he began his interrogation. It started with my family. This time I had prepared myself beforehand, aware of the possibility of an arrest, and so my story was a fluent one. My father, I told him, had been imprisoned by the French because of his outspoken pro-German attitude. 'I feel as German as you,' I went on, telling him how overjoyed I was that Alsace was once again part of the Fatherland.

'As a good German,' he said, 'you should go and work for the victory of the Reich in Germany, and leave this low life you have taken up.' I grinned sheepishly, compliantly, but my ordeal was far from over. Was the officer's friendliness merely an act, I wondered, designed to disarm and trap me? Now he turned in my direction the paper with the Hebrew characters on it. 'Do you know what these are?' he asked.

I lied at once. 'Oh, they're Greek or maybe Arabic letters.'

'No, you are wrong. These are Hebrew letters,' and he beamed as he spoke, like some grotesque caricature of a schoolmaster pleased to show off his knowledge to a favoured but idle pupil. Appearing to notice my nervous glances towards the human skull, he now turned to this object. He smiled again. 'This is the typical skull of a Jew,' he explained, adding that this was his special hobby. 'I have studied this subject closely, and I can accurately distinguish between the head of a Jew and a true Aryan.' He seemed very proud of this skill. He rose, looking at me again with deep concentration, then moved round the desk to stand behind me. As he took my head between his hands I felt his fingers start to trace, stop and trace again round the circumference of my skull with an obscene probing delicacy. Was I human, the questing fingers were assessing, or something other, something less than human? I was in a state of paralysed apprehension – from examining my head, I speculated, might he not move on, downwards, and require me to remove my trousers? The truth of my origins could then no longer be concealed. But instead he concluded his examination. 'Yes,' he declared, with a satisfied nod, 'I can feel that you have real German ancestry in your blood. I was almost sure of it from the moment I saw you.'

The interrogation was almost over, and my racial origins remained undetected through the man's belief in phrenology. But then he warned me, his voice coming to me through the fog of my fear, that he did not want to see me in Pigalle again. He returned to his desk and began laboriously writing on a sheet of paper. The scratching sound of his nib set my nerves on edge.

'This is the address of a German office which hires German-speaking people,' he announced at last, handing me the piece of paper. 'You will earn quite well and you will be together with your own people.'

I do not recall my exit from his office, only being out on the street once again, amid the crowds going about their business. I laughed to myself, nearly hysterical with relief. 'Look! Look!' I said to myself, 'now I'm a proper Aryan!'

I understood only one thing: that from this moment onwards it was too dangerous for me to continue working in Pigalle. I met Christos and Pierre at our bistro and told them what had happened. 'I know I have to leave,' I said.

'I'll go and see André,' said Pierre. 'He'll tell you what do to.'

'I'll have to keep away from Pigalle, too,' I added.

My time in Paris was drawing to a close. André was going to meet me in three days' time and meanwhile I went to see lots of films. Paris was a mecca of cinemas, but I don't remember the name of a single film I saw.

I met André, Christos and Pierre in the bistro at the appointed time. 'Now is your chance to fight the Germans properly,' said André. 'I am going to send you to some friends of mine in the South.' As much as I had enjoyed my time in Paris, I was excited at the prospect of fighting the enemy.

Once again I lay down in a room for what I knew would be the last time, with no certainty of what the future might bring me.

I embraced Christos before leaving. 'It was great,' he said, 'really great to have known you. Good luck, Robert.' I said the same to him, for it had been a marvellous adventure, and he and I had really become quite close.

Carrying my few belongings in my small suitcase, I left for the Gare d'Austerlitz and there bought a ticket for Figeac, a town in the south-west, the destination André had decided for me. The train pulled out of the station and soon the lights of Paris were extinguished in the darkness of the countryside.

5

FIGHTING BACK

THE DEMARCATION line between the Occupied and Unoccupied Zones of France had been dissolved on 11 November 1942. This meant that there were no routine checks at the former frontier and the train carrying me southwards continued without delay.

Figeac was in the *département* of Lot, and from there André had instructed me to travel to the village of Cardaillac. Figeac lies not far north of Gaillac, but by this time – it was now July 1943 – I had witnessed the *rafles* of Jews in Paris and knew that to mix with other Jews would be foolhardy. Being with my Jewish relatives in Gaillac – if they were still there – offered me no prospect of security. The bonds of family life which the Nazis had shattered had left me with confidence in only two resources: myself and my false papers. Nothing else, I was sure, would see me through.

I was pleased that I was no longer playing the part of the

enemy's good fellow, was no longer constrained to stand by and watch Jews rounded up. I would have happily spent the rest of the war in Paris, but now that this period of my life was over I was glad of it. I wanted only to fight the Germans and I did not care if I died in the effort.

André had told me to go to a restaurant called Chez Marcel and ask for Robert. With directions it was easy to find. The owner nodded when I mentioned Robert and at once made a telephone call.

Not long afterwards I heard the roar of a motorbike, and moments later a young man strode into the restaurant. He spoke to the owner, who indicated me with another nod. I mentioned the name André to the young man and, although he replied in a regional accent so strong I understood not a word, it was clear that I was to follow him. He attached my suitcase to the bike, mounted the machine, gestured for me to climb on, and make a circle of his arms to indicate I should hang on to him.

The engine burst into life and we sped off. I was thrilled by my first ride on a motorcycle. How I enjoyed the snarl of the engine and wild rushing of wind in my ears. The higher we climbed into the hills the more beautiful became the view of the valley as it fell away beneath us.

We stopped all too soon in a cluster of hills dotted with huts. My companion led me up to the one of the huts and knocked on the door. It was answered by an unsmiling, shortish, muscular character with a moustache as black as his beret, who led me inside. I heard the motorbike starting up again behind me. I shook hands with my new contact. His bearing was stiff and military, as befitted his words of introduction. 'I am Colonel Albert,' he said, indicating a chair. 'I am in charge of this group up here.' Then he began to question me. 'I have heard from André about you, but I want to hear your history from your lips. Start with your family background.' So I told my whole story again, with frequent interruptions from the Colonel for more detail. He seemed pleased when he heard about my membership of the Association of Socialist High School Students. He nodded when I told him that some of my family had been in Gaillac, not far from where we were. I said I had no idea what had happened to them, only that I had returned to Belgium and that my cousins Leo and Maxl had visited me in Paris on one occasion, despite the occupation. I also told him about my false papers.

Eventually, Colonel Albert seemed satisfied with my narrative. 'We are a small cell here. It is time for you to meet your group. Come with me.' His Resistance cell occupied three huts, and he led me to one of them, which was quite nearby. As soon as he entered, the men, who were sitting talking on straw pallets, immediately fell silent. It was clear that they respected their leader and were perhaps afraid of him.

'This is your new comrade, Robert,' said the Colonel. The six men all stood, murmured greetings and shook hands with me. I felt exhilarated to be counted a comrade, one of this little band of Resistance fighters. Later I learnt that we were part of the Francs-Tireurs et Partisans Français, one of the largest groups in the Maquis.

That night I ate with my new comrades. We cooked meat over a fire in our hut – a new experience for me, and how good it tasted – and each man told me his story. What a group we were, so much flotsam and jetsam thrown together by the war. There were two young people who did not want to go to Germany to labour in factories under the new law governing the Service du Travail Obligatoire (STO), which applied to unemployed Frenchmen between the ages of twenty-one and thirty-three. There were, like me, a few Jews – three I think – and a Catholic priest who had denounced the Nazis and had joined to avoid arrest.

So many stories, so many of which I have long since forgotten; but a few have remained in my memory. Young Jacques was a communist and the SS had come for him in his village in Brittany. He hid in a barn and watched as his parents were led from the house. The SS hit his mother, who cried out; his father rushed to protect her and they shot him on the spot. Another, older man, whose name I cannot remember, was also arrested as a communist, in his case a well-known one, a local leader. His torturers were not German but the Milice, the Vichy government police, who wanted names. This man showed me the deep scars on his legs and back where they had tied him naked to a wooden board, beaten him with a whip and poured scalding water on his wounds. He gave names to his tormentors in the end, but of people who had long since escaped to Spain.

There was a French Jew called Maurice, whose parents had been deported as Polish Nationals in a *rafle* in Paris. He had no idea what had become of them. Maurice and his brother fled Paris for the Unoccupied Zone. They hid in barns or with local people, but Maurice's brother was caught stealing from a farmer and turned over to the Milice. Maurice managed to escape. Another Jew, of about my age, called Armand Lipschitz, came from Limoges, where he had been a medical student. 'I worked part time in the Jewish community,' he told me. 'Limoges had quite a large Jewish community. After the Germans took over, a lot of us came down here. Anyway, in December 1942 the new law ordered us to have the word *"Juif"* attached to our identity papers and ration cards. I started producing false papers for Jews.

I was arrested in March 1943, caught red-handed with a number of sets of false papers.' He told me that friends managed to spirit him away, and so he ended up working with the Colonel.

Our hut was well placed on the top of a hill north-east of Figeac which gave us a view of the area below and the main road from Figeac to Rocamadour. We set up lookouts on the road to warn us of approaching German or Milice vehicles. I slept with my comrades on a straw pallet and we washed in a nearby stream. In the evening we moved around by candlelight.

Need was our only guide in the wooded hills. By day we did odd jobs on the surrounding farms for food and a little money. Some farmers who were sympathetic to the Resistance gave us supplies even when they had no work for us.

There were other farmers who were hostile to the Resistance. One of these, whose farm was near St Perdoux, stood out in his nastiness to us. He drove us away with curses. 'Bastards! Lazy communists!' he yelled after us, among other insults. Quite soon after I arrived there was a food shortage, and we plotted together without informing Colonel Albert. He was a dictator, and we knew he was unlikely to approve our decision to steal from the farmer at St Perdoux, so our plan appealed to us in three ways: as an act of defiance against the iron rule of the Colonel, as an act of revenge against the farmer and as a means of getting ourselves some meat.

There was no moon on the night we approached the farm armed with sharp knives and carrying sacks. We knew where the chicken coops and the rabbit hutches were. We split into two groups of three. We had to dispatch the animals efficiently and get away quickly before the farmer was disturbed by any noise. My group went for the rabbits, and one of my comrades whispered to me the way to kill one. I opened a hutch, grabbed a sleeping rabbit and, as directed, cut its throat with a single swift movement. Blood spurted all over me, but I found that I was not squeamish, and speedily threw the animal into my sack and ran off. It was a successful raid: we came away with two rabbits and three chickens. That night we enjoyed the meat, cooked on an open fire. These were strange and heady times, when theft seemed right and proper and I ate in the open air.

Sometimes the Colonel held political meetings in his hut, which we were expected to attend. He was a convinced communist and seemed to feel it his duty to indoctrinate us with his creed. Any emotional slack in his nature appeared entirely taken up by his political fervour and he would rage at any opposing view. Like most communists, he spoke in clichés, as if quoting from some textbook. 'After this war the communists will rule the world. Fascism is the last spasm of the old capitalist system. In the new world there will be no poverty because the wealth of the exploiters of the working class will be expropriated.' 'What about the pact Stalin made with Hitler?' someone once objected, to murmurs of agreement. 'Comrade Stalin,' replied the Colonel, raising his hands, 'needed a breathing space. That was only a temporary measure.'

I became friendly with the Colonel. Despite his austere manner, I liked him and never raised my voice in dissent at his political meetings. I saw him as a father figure, perhaps just because his strict ways reminded me of my own father. Perhaps he sensed I liked him and this was one of the reasons he made me his *agent de liaison*. 'Your German might come in useful if you are ever stopped. Your papers say you are from Alsace, so that if they stop you, you have your story,' he said when he explained my new duties to me. 'There are several groups of Resistance fighters up in these hills. Your job will be to take and bring back messages. Everything you see or hear is completely confidential. You discuss any such matters only with me.'

And so it was that I discovered the lovely villages and countryside of the region, either by bicycle, or on foot if my destination was in high terrain. I especially loved the villages of St Bressou and Le Bouyssou, with their beautiful little churches and houses decked out with baskets of flowers. I would hand over envelopes to various shadowy figures and return to our base with other envelopes.

Sometimes there would be missions for me to Rocamadour or Figeac, and then I would take the local bus. The gendarmes paid no heed to me, even if they might have suspected what I was up to. It was only the Milice I feared.

Once in a while the motorbike man, 'Robert', would turn up with a message, but he would never tarry.

Our group upped and moved around the hills from one camp to another, never remaining in one spot for long. We had very few weapons: some old revolvers, shotguns and our treasured weapon, a Sten gun which Colonel Albert taught us how to fire. He also instructed us in the use of explosives, but he never allowed us to handle them. We were all afraid of the Colonel, though we respected him because his disciplinarian ways instilled enough professionalism to make us something more than a ragbag of refugees and fugitives.

On a radio we listened to the BBC and followed the progress of the Allies, from the bombing of Rennes and Rouen to the capture of Tunis. Sometimes I would begin to brood and then I would withdraw from the others like a sick animal and find some

135

solitary place in the hills – there were plenty of these. Here I cried, asking myself what had become of my parents, wondering whether they had been forced to return to Poland, as the letter I received in Belgium had hinted. How ignorant I was in the ways of the Nazis to imagine that this was the worst that could happen to them. Then my ever-optimistic nature would reassert itself and I would assure myself that I would see my parents again when this nightmare was over. These lonely outbursts of emotion seemed to do me some good because my fighting spirit returned and I went back to my comrades full of renewed vigour. I knew that what our group was doing was small in the context of the war, but for me it was of tremendous importance. I was part of the Maquis and I was proud to be part of it.

One day Colonel Albert informed our cell that we were to blow up a German troop train which would pass through the area early the next morning on the main line to Figeac. At last we were going to engage the enemy with force. That night we scarcely slept, and it was still the early hours of the morning when Colonel Albert came for us. We travelled with another cell for about half an hour in a truck to the railway line, arriving at dawn. Members of cells rarely mingled with each other; I only knew the faces of the other Resistance fighters who were with us because in my role as *agent de liaison* I often ran messages from one cell to another.

The Colonel assigned roles to us – we were about twelve in all – but we were merely fetchers and carriers; it was Albert who attached the explosives to the line. This done, we lay in wait. As soon as we heard the train drawing near we ran into the cover of the hills behind us. From there we watched the flash and heard the explosion, saw the locomotive and wagons toppling off the track, an enthralling yet oddly remote spectacle, as if it were all some clever film effect. We made good our escape to some mountain caves about thirty kilometres away, knowing the Germans would soon be looking for us. We heard later that they had suffered some casualties, and had arrested ten people from surrounding villages, none of whom had anything to do with the sabotage.

Figeac held a market twice a week. I loved going there, simply to enjoy the hustle and bustle of normal life continuing despite the war. Peasants from neighbouring villages poured into the town to sell aubergines, carrots, tomatoes, spinach and cucumbers – all available without ration cards. Naturally there were shortages – in particular, eggs and chickens were strictly rationed – but in corners the black market operated unchecked, and one could buy almost anything there. The market reminded me of Vienna's Karmeliter Markt, where my mother used to take me on shopping expeditions. In the Figeac market I liked to wander among the stalls laden with cheap bric-a-brac. I lost myself gazing at the trashy treasures on display, old paintings, glassware, and carved wooden figures. The pall of war would lift and I could forget it or at least imagine that it had nothing to do with me.

On one of these trips I noticed a very pretty girl, with an abundance of rich, red hair. Her shirt, I noticed, was unbuttoned almost to her navel, the valley of her breasts easily visible every time she bent down. Perhaps I should have taken heed at this sort of display but, as it was, my head was turned and I didn't know which part of her to look at first, so I followed her. As she was all by herself and carrying a heavy shopping bag, I approached and offered my help. She smiled in acceptance, and I noticed the greenness of her eyes. She told me her name was Jacqueline and that she was shopping for her mother, who was unwell. I walked beside her and told her I was from Metz and worked for a farmer up on the hillside. We went to a bistro and I learnt that she had broken up with her boyfriend.

We started to meet in the evenings at a certain bistro and went for walks into the woods around Figeac. We made for an area called 'Le chemin des amoureux', or Lovers' Lane. Secluded by trees we lay down on the soft moss, warm from the intense summer heat, to make love. As in Paris, I preferred the dark and used a condom to hide the truth about myself. I thought it was love, with this very first girlfriend of my own age. In a weak moment I confided to Jacqueline that I was not working at a farm but was hiding on false papers because I did not want to go to Germany as a forced labourer.

Jacqueline was a moody girl and we had many fights. I found her headstrong, always wanting her own way. On one occasion we had arranged to meet at a bistro in Figeac but she stood me up. An hour later I ran into her at the market. 'I had other things to do,' she said. 'You're being childish.' 'And you are completely selfish,' I retorted. The argument grew heated and I turned and marched off. Some time later she apologised, but the seeds of our failure had been sown. When I decided to end things between us I tried to do so gently, but Jacqueline raged at me and we had our final battle. I had taken my pleasure with her, she accused me, because she was good enough for that, and now I was leaving her with no consideration for her feelings at all. She slapped my face, spat at me and left. I felt only relief.

A week later Albert told me to take a message to another Resistance group, this one in Bergerac. This meant taking a train. I am clear about the date, because it was my mother's birthday, 5

August 1943, and I thought of her a great deal on that day. I was quietly settled in a compartment with some farmers and their families, when the train suddenly came to a halt. I thought nothing of this until I saw the black-uniformed Milice surrounding the train. My heart started to pump wildly and I was only glad that I was not carrying an incriminating document but instead on my way to collect something. Yet I was concerned about my false papers. I had a premonition that things were going to turn out badly for me today, as if I knew that I had exhausted my store of good luck. The Milice entered our carriage and asked for everyone's papers. One of them – an officer, I think – took mine and consulted a book he was carrying, looked at me with a slow smile and ordered me to follow him. I was put into a covered truck with several other young people and we were taken to the police station at Figeac and locked in a cell for the night, with bare boards to sleep on.

I kept thinking about that notebook the Milice officer had consulted. What could his smile have meant other than that he had found my name there? Had I been betrayed? Who had known of my false name, other than Colonel Albert and my comrades? Suddenly I thought of Jacqueline's rage when we had parted. She knew that my papers were false. My suspicions attached themselves to her and I berated myself for my foolish pillow talk.

The next morning another Milice officer interrogated me. He had my identification papers in front of him. He shouted at me, 'We know your papers are false, we know you are part of a terrorist group. Before I start breaking your jaw, give me your name and who you are working for.' He stood, with a fierce expression on his face, menacingly clenching and unclenching his

139

fists. 'I am not a terrorist!' I shouted back, but this only maddened him and he struck me hard in the face. Blood streamed down my shirt as he yelled, 'We know this is not your real name! Tell us what it is and the names of those in your Resistance group! We can make you tell us!' He hit me again with his fist and I fell, hitting my head against the wall. I must have fainted, because I remember coming round to cold water splashing in my face. I made a calm decision. I knew of the brutal methods of the Milice. I did not want to betray anybody, or to suffer more. So I made a confession and announced, 'I am an Austrian Jew from Vienna called Alfred Knoller, I am hiding from the Germans, and have nothing to do with any Resistance group.' The officer looked stunned, stared at me for a moment, turned on his heel and soon I heard him on the telephone in the next room. He then drove me to Gestapo headquarters, where I repeated my story. The next day I was interrogated by the Gestapo. I gave a vague and misleading story as to how I came by my false papers.

To this day I cannot help but believe it was Jacqueline who betrayed me, though the way the Milice officer on the train smiled knowingly at my papers might have been simply because they showed me to be eligible for the STO. But, if so, what was the purpose of the book he carried? Perhaps I am wrong about Jacqueline, and these costly forgeries were just not as good as I thought they were.

Jacqueline may still be alive. Only she knows the truth, and it will probably die with her. In any event, how was she to know that her betrayal of me, if betray me she did, was to lead me straight to Auschwitz? The exact circumstances surrounding my arrest – the beginning of my real ordeal – will always remain a mystery.

I was put under armed guard and taken by train back to Paris, and from there to Drancy, in the quiet suburb of Bobigny, the assembly camp for deportation to the East.

6

DRANCY

THE CAMP at Drancy was the antechamber to some other destination – nobody knew where, only that it was in the East. 'We'll be going to Germany,' some said, while others said, 'No, Poland.' It took the imagination of children to name this shadowy region. 'Pitchipoi,' they called it in their piping voices. '*Pitchipoi! Pitchipoi!*' A marvellous and terrifying nonsense word for the unknown.

Members of the efficient Garde Mobile escorted eleven of us into Drancy. The French policemen led us across a vast courtyard filled with milling civilians, whose absent yet watchful manner filled me with anxiety. Except for the machinery designed to keep me a prisoner here – the watchtowers, the coils of barbed wire, the men in uniforms – Drancy looked like nothing more than some vast, cheaply built apartment block.

We were deposited in an office, where, behind some tables, sat some men with the yellow star on their breast pocket, while unobtrusively in the background stood an SS man. These prisoners wore, in addition to the star, white armbands bearing the initials 'MS'. I realised that this represented some kind of authority and I quickly discovered that they were '*Membres de Service*', Jews appointed by the Germans to administer their own people.[1] The MS even appointed Jewish policemen to maintain order in the camp.

As my turn for registration drew near I saw some of the men in front of me surrender small valuables, mostly watches, wedding rings, sometimes money, to the MS. The official scribbled on a piece of paper, which he then handed over, with the warning, 'Don't lose this receipt!' The property was deposited in bags. My turn came to step forward. The MS recorded my name and place of origin. He glanced at my clothing and I did not at first understand that he was checking to see if I bore the yellow star. He produced one and handed it to me. 'Have it sewn on your clothes,' he told me. 'If you have any valuables, you may deposit them now, it is up to you. There is thieving in this camp.' Apart from the clothes I arrived in, I had nothing except my watch and a tiny amount of money, and I declared that I would retain these. The MS nodded. 'If you see a German officer, you must stop and stand to attention until he has passed. Do you understand?' I nodded and he looked beyond me to the person next in line.

I held the rough piece of cloth bearing that emblem of identity I had seen so often on the Paris streets: the yellow star, embossed at its centre with the single, black-lettered word 'Juif'. I had managed to evade that identity for so long that I had felt I was safe from it. But now it was as if the enemy had seized me roughly by the shoulder and was saying, 'Wake up, fool! You have been dreaming. Did you think you could get away with it? We know what you are! And in case you forget this star will be there to remind you.' All the same, I experienced a strange relief to have my faith back again. The burden of guilt I had gained during my days in Paris was now lifted. And in the back of my mind I was sure that my dear parents would also be wearing the yellow star. I felt almost defiant, as I had in Vienna, when I had decided that since I was defined as a Jew by the gentiles, then I would take that as my identity and not an Austrian one.

I made my way back to the vast courtyard, melting into the mass there. I was full of questions. In a new place one needed knowledge. 'Mind out for Brunner, and the Boxer,' one inmate warned.[2] Brunner was the Commandant, he told me, a brutal man. 'This boxer?' I asked, 'was he some German champion before or something?' The man explained, 'We call him "the Boxer" because he likes to punch people.'

I was forced to adjust to my stark new reality when later a woman in the camp sewed the yellow star on to the breast pocket of my jacket. I understood that I could no longer think in terms of how I might act because now I was merely one of the herded thousands wearing the star.

I slept in a large room with two rows of double-tiered wooden bunks set so close together that there was scarcely room to set down your belongings. I was glad I had so few.

There was no work for us here. There was gardening if you wanted to do it, but nobody compelled you. We wrote letters and played cards in rooms on the ground floor, where there were tables and chairs. We ate the inadequate food they gave us, coffee, bread, margarine and a little jam in the morning, soup at lunchtime and in the evening. Speculation and argument filled our discussions. I joined in because there was nothing else to do save wait upon the German decree. And their decree was the lists.

The lists! You never knew when the next one would be pinned to the board in the administration building, but word spread like wildfire when it was. There was no chance of missing your name up there among the next one thousand to be deported – there were always one thousand names – because the lists were in alphabetical order. My only difficulty was that my poor eyesight forced me to stand close to the board to make out the letters.

Some, especially those who had been arrested and ill-treated by the police in the *rafles*, did not believe a word of the official line given us: 'You will work in our factories! We need your skills! Anyone who is a carpenter or a builder or a watchmaker will be useful to us! And for the others, we will find work!' I could not share their pessimism. I was just not made that way. 'They will kill us,' these people said. Others argued against this. 'Haven't they given us receipts for our property? Surely, with their own people fighting, they will indeed need our skills? Not even the Nazis would kill children.' Others talked of escape. 'Are you crazy? They kill people who try that!' 'How do you know that?' others would counter. There was no proof, but the mere possibility filled us with dread and kept most of us docile.

Even the actions of the small SS command at Drancy could not compare with the quiet bureaucratic menace of the lists, because the SS were merely the flesh-and-blood part of the machinery. If one avoided them, one was reasonably safe. Occasionally I saw Brunner, his face expressionless beneath his SS cap. I hardly dared look at him in case his eye fell on me. One day, though, I was able to watch him from the safety of a crowd. He stuck a knife in the ground, pointed his stick at a man and shouted. The man came forward and Brunner barked at him again. The poor fellow, who perhaps had forgotten to stop when

Brunner approached, started running round the knife and every time he passed Brunner, the Commandant struck him with his stick. It was now that I at last saw an expression in Brunner's eyes, the fixed expression of a person intent only on inflicting more and more pain until the need to inflict it has been sated. The victim of Brunner's sadism soon fell exhausted to the ground.

Brückler had won his nickname 'the Boxer' not only because of his predilection for punching people, but also because he habitually wore a boxing glove on his right hand to do this. I once witnessed him exercise his skill with his glove when he punched a woman to the ground and calmly walked on. 'The Boxer' needed no reasons for punching, he just liked doing it.

On another occasion the entire camp was ordered to watch two men beat each other twenty-five times with sticks, their punishment for trying to smuggle messages out of the camp. Brunner pronounced the sentence, and afterwards the two men were dragged away to an underground bunker.

There were suicides at Drancy. I witnessed the aftermath of two, saw the crowds gather around the still shapes on the ground. Drancy was an ideal place for such actions. Nobody was there to stop a person climbing to the highest floor and leaping off.

But I was young. And, like all the young, I believed myself to be immortal. The effect upon me of the star I now bore faded somewhat. They would never get me, I firmly believed. The SS were just pathological criminals drunk with power, no more, I told myself. I would not die like these poor suicides, nor would I find my name on any lists. How often had I run to the administration building to check the new lists? Countless times. And every time I had turned away, seeing around me the stony, expressionless faces of those chosen, and only exulting that I had

147

not been selected. I lived in such hope, dread and denial all my time at Drancy.

The person in the bunk next to me was a boy of about my own age. He was from Germany, and his name was Bernard, but we called him Bernie. We fell in together and he introduced me to his mates, also German. We fooled around together, and it took the edge off my anxiety to be with people of my own age. One day we were messing around in a basement area. 'Hey! Come over here!' cried one of our number as he jumped up and down on a concrete slab. 'Listen to that!' he exclaimed, drawing our attention to the hollow sound it made. We gathered around and managed to lift the slab to one side. We gazed in astonishment at an excavated area underneath. It was the beginnings of a tunnel, no more than five metres long, and leading towards the wall adjoining the barbed-wire fence. It appeared quite fresh. Despite the danger, we decided to work on the tunnel. Telling nobody else of our find we worked night and day, hoping to complete the tunnel before the next list. We had poor tools, and moving the earth to sites where it would not be noticed was hard work, so progress was very slow.

The task was, in truth, almost impossible, and perhaps we knew this in our hearts. But it felt better to do something, anything, rather than play cards, debate our fate and have one's mind fixed only on the next list. In the end it was fortunate for us that it was only the Jewish police who discovered our activities. 'Are you mad? If the Germans had found you, you would be dead!' They dragged us away from the tunnel, extinguishing our foolish dream of escape.

It was on 5 October 1943 that the list with my name was pinned up on the board. I stared, as if my eyes might be deceiving me, but they had not, and now it was I who became one of the stony faces.

As I turned away I found myself looking at a face I did not know. We smiled at each other in a resigned way which communicated that we were both named, and became friends almost at once. It turned out we were both from Vienna, and from the same district.

'But why are you called Pierre?' I asked the young man.

'Oh, I was Peter Heimrath, but I got out and went to Marseilles, and became Pierre. I love Marseilles, I could have stayed the rest of my life,' he said, his expression one of fond recollection.

Pierre impressed me immediately. He had dark good looks and a toothy, ready smile. His skin was smooth, which accentuated his high cheekbones. I felt I would not go wrong sticking with him because he seemed much more worldly-wise than me.

'What did you like so much about Marseilles?' I asked.

He smiled again. 'The food, and the women,' he replied. 'What these French don't know about food ... I learnt to cook, you know, make bouillabaisse. Those women ... beautiful.'

'Tell me about them,' I said.

And how Pierre regaled me on that last day in Drancy with tales of his adventures with women. I was an eager and credulous audience, though his looks and charm made it easy to believe in his success. I looked up to him, and laughed when he told me over and over again, like a line from a chorus, 'I change women like my socks.' Perhaps there was more to my admiration of Pierre than his worldliness, some sense which told me that here was a born survivor. A man who could so easily move from Austria to France, from Peter to Pierre, so easily slough off one woman for the next – such a man's very inconstancy, even shallowness, might be the very qualities one would need in the place where we were bound.

I told Pierre about our tunnel. 'I wish I had known about it,' he said.

Back in my dormitory the troubled face of Bernie told me that he, too, was on the list.

We assembled on 6 October in the main square, were checked and given a piece of bread and margarine for the journey. The Jewish administration had issued me with warm clothes, and these I put in the single suitcase which the rules allowed each person to take.

I managed to sit with Pierre, guarded by SS and gendarmes, on the bus, which took us to a rail depot somewhere not far from the camp, though I had no idea where. The station platform to which we had been brought was screened off, which filled me with alarm. I saw SS men carrying whips and accompanied by dogs. There seemed to be hundreds of us on the platform, but the Germans created order.[3] They counted and separated us into rows in front of windowless trucks, that had barbed wire drawn across the narrow openings at the top. The trucks had been used to transport men or horses to the Front. I managed to read the legend on the side of one: '*40 hommes ou 8 chevaux*' ('Forty men or eight horses'). Pierre and I started talking about escaping from the train. Such talk gave us hope.

SS men moved forward and rolled open the sliding doors. I looked around at the many people in my section and then again at the truck, meant for this maximum of forty persons. Was this possible? So many in so small a space? For the Germans, there was a financial reckoning behind the gross overcrowding in the trucks: the railway company had to be paid for our transportation. Then came shouts from the SS. Everyone hesitated, but the SS drove us forward under their whips. Our orderly rows at once dissolved into a scrambling mass of terrified human beings struggling towards the mouth of the truck. I was pushed on by the people behind me and I pushed against those in front of me, not caring whether it was a man, woman or child, but wanting only to avoid the whips of the Nazis.

I looked round for Pierre as I clambered into the truck, but there was no sight of him. The chaos greeting me inside was much more terrible than that outside. Some, presumably the first into the truck, had already sat down with their families. There were angry shouts and the cries of babies in arms as people fought and pushed one another aside. I ended up in a tiny space opposite the doors. Yet still there was light, the doors were drawn back, I could see a part of the world outside. But the SS men stepped forward and rolled the doors shut. The previous shouts of anger turned into screams of terror, and I joined others in banging my fists against the imprisoning wooden walls. I thought I would go mad in this confinement. My chest soon heaved with the exhaustion caused by my exertions, an almost welcome limpness overcame me and I sank into myself.

A strident voice now blared from a loudspeaker:

'You are being sent to a place where you will work for the glory of the Reich! Families will remain together and all those capable of working will be given work. Your train journey will last approximately two days. Anyone attempting to escape will be shot! You must all prevent escapes, because if anyone attempts to escape the whole wagon will be severely punished.'

The train jolted forward, and meagre rays of light began to filter through the narrow openings in the truck as we left the station. And then out of this confusion came a strong, loud voice. I looked to where it came from and managed to see that the man speaking, who stood near a wall of the truck, was someone I had known a little at the camp. 'We must sort ourselves out, we cannot all sit on the floor, that must be clear to you. If we don't organise ourselves we will not survive this journey.' This was a voice of someone whose mind retained clarity, who was willing to take responsibility for us, to risk hostility in this stifling hell. He went on to advise that sitting space should be for the old, the infirm and nursing mothers, and that everyone else should alternately stand and sit every two hours during the day, and every three hours at night. People did listen to him, and so our self-appointed organiser managed to make things slightly more tolerable for us in our packed prison.

Even so, it was not long before the rank smell of humanity became a stench. How could it be otherwise, when there was only one bucket for sanitary needs? In fact there were soon two, as there was another bucket, full of water, which quickly became empty. Before long both buckets were overflowing with urine and excrement and our faces reflected despair, disgust and hopelessness, because there was no alternative to relieving oneself directly on to the floor. 'The floorboards!' cried our organiser. 'We can cut through and empty the buckets, and the men can also urinate there.' People produced small knives, scissors, whatever implements they had, and soon a small hole appeared. Other voices, young in the main, now made themselves heard. 'If we make the hole big enough we can escape.' I joined in with these voices. If I could only get out of this train, I was sure my luck would seem me through. Whatever was out there could be no worse than the horror inside. But the older people, the larger number, were resolutely against escape. 'You are crazy!' they cried, their voices full of fear. 'You heard what the Germans said, they will kill you if you are caught and punish the rest of us! Besides we are too old to escape, we will be the ones punished for your actions.' In the event our small and blunt implements proved almost useless against the solid planks of the floor, and the hole we made was only large enough for the men to urinate through.

Despite the efforts of our organiser, our journey East was filled with irritable arguing over space. I and others joined him in his efforts to induce calm, but my attempts to reason with people were usually greeted with abuse. Even the periods of exhausted silence were interrupted by the loud praying of the religious, which set my teeth on edge. Then I turned my eyes away in shame, and saw other men do the same, as one mother after another was forced to satisfy her baby's hunger in front of us. Public breastfeeding was unknown at that time.

I lost all sense of time, bringing myself back from whatever world I managed to lose myself in only to listen to the debates which intermittently sprang up. A middle-aged man standing near me, whose appearance and perfect German were those of an academic, began to declaim, 'The Nazis are treating us as they think befits our status in their eyes, as *Untermenschen*. Therefore we must prove them wrong by never relinquishing our moral standards. Even in these dire circumstances we must ensure that our intellect prevails, so that we may emerge a people of dignity and moral standing.' A young man near him, unable to contain himself, shouted angrily across this address, 'You do not know what you are talking about with your "proving them wrong". Do you think to win their respect? Ha! They are not interested in any *example* from us. They want to rid the world of all of us. *Mein Kampf* makes this perfectly clear. Have you not read that worthy document? The Nazis shout, "*Juda Verrecke*" and they are doing their best to make that a reality. Is this truck not proof enough for you? I say, then, to hell with your decency and moral upbringing. The moral life is dead, dead, don't you see that? We must do anything to keep alive, even steal from each other. It is the only hope. It is every man for himself. The world has no idea what they are doing to us. We must escape and announce the truth. That is all we can hope to do.'

The academic-looking man looked appalled. Voices, including mine, were raised in protest against the young man. 'You are crazy,' I told him. 'You have no right to upset people with these words. Haven't we receipts for our things? They need us, after all – their young men are in the army. We must struggle to remain human beings, and come out of this as such. The Allies are in Sicily, Mussolini is finished, the Russians have halted the German offensive...' And so I went on, hopeful as always.

Before long I had taken to looking after an older man who happened to sit next to me and who reminded me of my father. I created extra room for him, keeping people at a distance from the kindly gentleman. I told him my life story and he smiled gently, seeming to take in every word. He succeeded in bolstering my spirits. 'Freddie, you are young, you have your whole future. Don't be afraid, or give up hope, ever. We must remain in good heart to stay alive. The Nazis will never get rid of us, never.' Robert Waitz was his name and he was a doctor from Paris. I knew nothing else about him then. Sitting near us was a poor man wheezing dreadfully, an asthmatic whose frequent attacks were no doubt aggravated by the conditions in the train. Robert looked at him with deep concern, and eventually gave him a pill, 'to help him sleep', he told me. Next morning the man, no older than the doctor, was dead, and I have always wondered about the contents of that pill. The asthmatic now joined the other dead, whom we had piled up near the doors. Most of these deceased were elderly people who lacked the strength to stand the ordeal any longer.

As time passed the stench inside the truck worsened with the odour of the bodies and because some among us developed diarrhoea and were unable to reach the bucket. I, like everyone else, was tortured with thirst.

At some point on the second day the train stopped. The doors rolled back, revealing an anonymous scene of fields. I saw SS men appearing at the door, so I assumed we were in Germany, though this was of no interest to me. One of them pointed to two of our number who happened to be near the doors, ordering them to pick up the buckets and follow him. The two men left the truck with the overflowing, stinking buckets, and the SS detailed others nearby to remove the dead bodies. A trolley appeared outside pulled by some other prisoners and they loaded the bodies on to this and moved off with it. I was merely relieved that the bodies were gone, as this afforded me slightly more room. The poor asthmatic man was for me – if I thought about him at all – now merely one of those bodies trundled away.

Eventually the two prisoners returned with the buckets, both filled with water. I remember that we had some small containers of some kind, which somebody in the truck must have provided. Our organiser took command of the buckets and filled the containers as they were passed forward in the still-crowded truck. Water had never tasted so sweet in my throat as on that day.

The doors rolled shut once more. As the train moved on,

darkness fell. I felt exhausted and this exhaustion helped me to sleep and so forget thirst and hunger.

There were occasional further stops when the doors remained closed. Once again we had no water, so we called out loudly. I could hear German voices outside, some sounding curious, and then shouts, presumably of SS men, ordering the owners of these voices to stand back from the train.

The train continued on its journey and the temperature in the truck plummeted. It snowed, and we held out containers, pieces of cloth, anything to catch a few drops of moisture. Our young organiser ensured that everyone received a little liquid. I knew this young man's name then, but I have completely forgotten it now.

Once, rising over the perpetual bickering, a single anguished woman's cry silenced us. 'My baby, my baby, she is not moving. Help me! Help me!' My new friend Robert Waitz got up and went to the child. 'The baby is dead,' he said in a low voice. The mother screamed again, wanting to hold on to her child. But finally she surrendered the baby to a bearded religious man, who took the infant in his arms and recited a prayer. He covered the baby with a prayer shawl from his suitcase. The entire wagon then recited the Jewish prayer for the dead. This ancient Jewish ritual briefly brought us all together.

How long had we been travelling? I did not know. Where were we? I did not know. All I knew was that it was bitterly cold.

At last the train stopped. The doors of the wagons slammed back, admitting a cold, blinding light such as I had never experienced before. I saw more SS men with dogs. They clapped their hands to their faces because of the stench coming from us. In a stupor of exhaustion, we stumbled from the train at their order, though some in the truck could scarcely move. I heard a voice from a loudspeaker, which urged us to remain calm:

'Welcome to *Arbeitslager* Auschwitz. You have had a rough few days in the train. But now you have arrived at your destination! Please descend from your truck and line up. Take only your most important belongings with you and leave the heavy cases in the wagon. You will receive them later in the camp. You will be temporarily separated. Women and old people and children will be transported by lorry into the camp. Men will walk to the camp. You will be reunited later. There will be work for all of you. For those unable to work in the factories there will be gardening and light tasks. Everyone must obey the instructions of the officer as to who will walk and who will take the lorry. The faster this is done the sooner you will drink and eat!'

Not so bad then, I thought, my spirits reviving slightly despite my exhaustion and the bitter chill of the air. These Germans were tough, yes – I saw them cuff a few people slow to descend, usually old people they should not have cuffed – but they were not exactly brutal. There would be work for us after all. To my surprise I heard a German voice calling out, 'Professor Waitz! Professor Robert Waitz! Please come forward!' I had no idea that my friend was a professor, distinguished enough for the Germans to single him out.

My thoughts were interrupted by a strange new sight. People in dirty striped garments and matching caps moved forward through our line. They took some people out of the wagons, then removed the baggage from inside and piled it some distance away from us.[4] The woman with the dead baby screamed hysterically to an SS man, 'My baby is dead! My baby is dead!' and he directed her to the lorries and her own death.

157

An SS officer selected those of us who were to walk to the camp. I was glad to see Robert nearby, and we marched together towards the camp. This march lasted about fifteen minutes, until I saw from afar the gate and its inscription: '*Arbeit Macht Frei*', a sentiment whose hollowness was revealed by the barbed wire all around and the men in their machine-gun watchtowers.

It was the peculiar sound of music that greeted us, played by musicians in the same odd pyjamas. SS officers waited for us at the entrance.

This was Pitchipoi, our new home.

7

PITCHIPOI

EVERY EVENT in my story leads up to Auschwitz and no subsequent thought or action in my life is untouched by the memory of Auschwitz. To this day, to my dear wife's consternation, I gobble food as if there might never be any more, and when my own plate is empty I look at hers.

The person who stumbled into the cattle truck at Drancy lost once and for all his youthfulness, if not all his naivety. The Nazi machinery of degradation started for me in the packed cattle wagon and though this experience was only an introduction to Auschwitz it was an instructive, even useful one.

I was so exhausted on arrival at the camp that I hardly took in how bizarre it was to be greeted with music. Here were black-uniformed SS men and watchtowers dominating a vast enclosure defined by barbed wire.

As we passed through the gate a person in the pyjamas, who was standing near the SS men and wore an armband marked with the word '*Kapo*', shouted, '*Mützen ab!*' Hats off!' and knocked the hat off the head of a middle-aged man slow to obey the order. We were marched past long low buildings to a large square area, the *Appellplatz*, or assembly area, where we were halted and pushed into rows of five.

Here a prisoner of an altogether different appearance addressed us. He also wore the pyjamas, but it was on a stylish windcheater that I saw displayed a green triangle beneath a number on a white strip. He addressed us loudly in German. 'I am your *Lagerälteste* [camp commandant]. You are in *Arbeitslager* [work camp] Buna, part of the Auschwitz concentration camp. You are here to work and obey...'

It was hard to stand to attention, hard to listen properly in my condition. But the harsh voice continued its speech of induction, barking out a list of things that would now happen to me. I would be registered, and then undergo delousing, because they did not want my filthy lice in this camp. I would be showered, have my head shaved, be tattooed. At the end of this, and only at the end, I might do the one thing I craved: eat and drink.

The voice stopped and then there was silence and a thousand souls stood in the assembly area as dead as stones. My resource was the trick I had learnt in the wagon, simply to shut down and wait passively for the next thing to happen. In that state I could perhaps have endured a lengthy wait in the square, I do not know; but finally came another voice, announcing that registration would begin. Because there were so many of us, it took some time before the shuffling movement trickled back to my rank and I followed a line of men to the front of a building near to the entrance of the camp. When my turn came I entered a room and stood before a prisoner seated at a table, a Jew or a political prisoner, I cannot remember which. He had a list and asked me for my name and date of birth, and, I think, my place of birth. It was the last time here that I would be identified by them as a person. He checked the information against his list. 'Do you have a profession or a trade?' he asked.

'No, I was a student, that's all.' A bad answer.

The prisoner scribbled something on his list and ordered me to the adjacent block, where a '2' was displayed outside.

I fell into a scene of chaos and humiliation. A prisoner waved a stick furiously. 'Filthy Jews! Strip off! Leave your clothes on the floor, but tidily! Leave everything in your pockets and don't think to hide anything! We will find it and beat the daylights out of you!' I stripped naked with the others and stood ashamed among them. I glanced around and saw Pierre. We moved close to each other. 'Let's stick together,' I said. He nodded. The harsh voice of the prisoner interjected. 'Jews! Run to the next block for delousing! Fast!'

We ran to another section within the block. Here other prisoners sprayed us with stinking chemicals and painted our bodies with white stuff, and then more men with *Kapo* armbands drove our naked bodies outside into the freezing air. They herded the mass of us through the compound and into another block. We huddled together for warmth and suddenly water poured down over us, which we immediately started to gulp. But they scarcely gave us enough time even for that. The showers dried up and with blows and shouts of '*Raus!*' and '*Schnell!*' they drove us outside again, the water on my body only increasing the renewed shock of the cold air.

I found myself back in Block 2, where a line of prisoners placidly awaited our group with scissors and razors. I heard some of our older members try to make conversation with them as we sat down to be stripped of our hair. 'Where are our wives, our children?' they asked. 'Forget about them,' the barbers replied, 'as you will not see them again. They are dead, and their souls are on the way to heaven via the chimney.' Pierre and I looked at each other in disgust at these remarks, while others attacked the barbers for their poor sense of humour. Yet I observed with apprehension how indifferent the barbers were to these criticisms. I sat in a chair when my turn came and submitted to their instruments.

I stood in line once more as I passed through to yet another section of the block. Here more prisoners stood, armed with short electric needles. I tried to talk to the one who took my left arm. He worked swiftly, mechanically, looking only at my arm. 'Are you Jewish?' I asked him. 'No, I am a political prisoner, from Poland,' he replied. I had seen the red triangle on his breast, with the letter 'P', but did not yet understand its meaning. The tool worked away, creating numbers on my forearm. 'This is you now – 157103. You will not be called by your name, only by this number.'

It was strange to feel the cold biting into my hairless skull as they drove us to another block, this one displaying the number '54'. How indistinguishable we all looked! No clothes. No hair. Just shivering, pink creatures.

We seemed to wait for some time outside this block, the *Kleider Kammer*, the clothing store. Finally I was summoned in with nine or ten others and two prisoners inside looked us up and down as if assessing our size and height. There was a group of long benches in this room. The prisoners then handed each of us a pile of the pyjama-like clothes and crude wood and canvas shoes. 'Go to the benches and dress!' ordered the Kapos. We obeyed, but waves of laughter followed as we realised how hopelessly ill fitting these garments were. A particularly loud outburst of mirth followed my clown's performance as I stood up and my trousers fell down. When I put the shoes on I discovered that they were both for the left foot. I looked around, hoping to find someone with a pair of right shoes. I took the strings from one of the shoes and tied it as a belt round my waist. I found the man with the two right shoes but, of course, he would not accept the stringless left shoe from me, and I was fortunate to find an abandoned piece of the stuff in a corner.

The *Kapos* lined us up, and it was a new and surprisingly young voice which now ordered us out of the building. My eyes fell on a prisoner of no more than fourteen years old. '*Raus!*' he called, and I instinctively dreaded this good-looking youth, fearing the caprice of a young person with power over his elders. We followed this boy a short distance into a block designated as number 53. '*Line up over there!*' bellowed the lad, and I found myself facing the entrance of a smallish room. This was the *Tagesraum*, the day room used by the *Blockälteste* (block senior) and his cronies, and it was also where food was dished out. Pierre's proximity was a great comfort to me.

The entrance to this room now framed the shape of a broad-shouldered and brutal-looking man. Although he wore pyjamas, I observed how well cut, even elegant, his were. He also bore the green triangle on his breast, indicating that he was a German criminal. The man boomed at us. '*Franzosen* [Frenchmen], I am your *Blockälteste* and these' – he pointed to a pair of truncheons hanging on the wall behind him – 'are my helpers. I will use these if I have any trouble with you. You live eat and sleep in this barrack. Choose a sleeping partner – you sleep two in a bunk, head to the feet of your partner. You will now get your spoon and bowl. You will receive no replacement for any lost item, not a bowl, not a spoon, not a shoe. Take your eyes from them for a second and they will disappear. You are all thieves. I advise you to tie the bowl around your waist, and keep the spoon in your pocket.' I quickly understood the simple law pertaining here: no bowl, no food. I did not think what it might mean to lose a shoe, because all I was thinking about was food.

They gave us each our *Schüssel* – the all-important metal bowl – and a spoon. Throughout this introductory speech the smell of food rising from a great cauldron beside the *Blockälteste* tormented me. I could think of little else except getting something in my mouth. For this I felt I would do anything. 'Line up!' called the *Blockälteste*, 'and you will call out your number as you take your ration!' I took my place in a queue, which now moved forward at what seemed to me an agonisingly slow pace. Behind the cauldron stood somebody who distributed a ladleful into each proffered bowl. 'One five seven one zero three!' I said as I reached him, and he dipped his ladle into a watery substance and filled my bowl. I moved away and swallowed the soupy liquid as quickly as possible, tasteless as it was.

The faces of the older men, the ones with families, were set in deep apprehension. A middle-aged man standing near to me and Pierre gave way to tears. 'Where could they be?' he asked pleadingly, as if I might have the answer. 'I have a wife and a child, three years old.' He shook his head. I put my arm around the man in sympathy. 'From now on,' I urged him, 'act only upon what your eyes see, tell yourself not to give up and think only to stay alive at all costs.' This was small comfort to the man, who merely stared ahead.

Next to me stood another prisoner, with the same red triangle on his pyjamas as the man who had tattooed me. As mysterious as this symbol still was to me, the significance of the tattooed number did not even occur to me. The lower the number on your arm the longer you had been in Auschwitz. I quickly learnt to treat such prisoners, who had survived so long, with respect. They were often privileged in the system and had a certain influence. There were even Jews here who, if they had been in Auschwitz for a long time, wore the red triangle of their political dissidence and not a star. These individuals, too, were privileged. So my question to this prisoner with a red triangle was a reasonable one. I asked him, as I had the man who had tattooed me, whether he was Jewish. His expression was much more kindly than that of the tattooist, but his answer was similar, as he explained that he was from Poland, a political prisoner. 'My name is Tadek,' he said. He spoke perfect German and appeared altogether such a gentle and well-educated person that I asked him another question. 'Do you know what has happened to all the missing ones here? People are wondering about their families?'

Tadek replied, 'Nobody here knows anything, but whenever there is a new transport, well, the air smells differently, sickly sweet, burning. The belief among us is that they are killing women and old people, perhaps children, too, and burning them. I mean, look around, even if they are taking the women and children somewhere else, you don't see any old men here, do you? Look, don't repeat what I have said...'

But rumour soon filled the block as insidiously as the smell Tadek had spoken about. There were religious people among us who had arrived with their large families, and they started to cry out, wail and beat their chests. They faced East and chanted Kaddish, the Jewish prayer for the dead. Pierre, goaded into a frenzy, shouted at them, 'Stop praying for the dead! They are not served by your prayers! We must be strong, otherwise we'll follow them.' I and others shouted our agreement, but one of the religious retorted, 'We will only live if God wants us to.' 'Did God want to kill the children?' Pierre yelled back. There never was and never will be any meeting point for such opposing views of the world.

One of the *Blockälteste's* assistants, a *Stubendienst*, oversaw us as we chose our bunks. It was natural that I shared with Pierre. We were given the middle one, vertically between two others, covered with a thin straw mattress, two straw pillows and two blankets. I was so exhausted I could have slept in more uncomfortable places than this. Besides, Pierre and I were of a similar slight build – a considerable advantage in such a small space. 'I advise you to wrap your *Schüssel* and spoon in your shirt and sleep on them if you don't want them stolen!' the *Blockälteste* had warned. We did so, placing them under our pillow. I fell asleep at once.

A shouted word, repeated over and over, drove into my unconsciousness. '*Aufstehen! Aufstehen*! Get up!' I tried to, but could not. Then someone was shaking me insistently. A voice close to my ear called urgently, 'Wake up, Freddie! Wake up!' I opened my eyes and saw Pierre staring at me. He was already half dressed. All around me men were quickly dressing. I got out of the bunk, remembering to tie the *Schüssel* around my waist and put the spoon in my trouser pocket.

We were led outside in the dark to an open-air washing facility. There was a round bowl with six taps, and here we formed a queue. We moved forward quite quickly, but I was cold and impatient. Spotting an identical basin set apart, I bypassed the

166

queue and went and stripped in front of this one. No sooner had I started washing than I was seized violently and a ferocious blow landed full in my face. My glasses smashed and fell to the ground. A *Kapo* shouted, 'This basin is for *Kapos* only, you dirty Jew!' Blood streamed from my nose. I stood shaking with shock and once again it was Pierre who came to my rescue. He led me back to our basin and applied cold water to my neck. 'You are a fool, Freddie, a real fool,' he chided. 'What did you imagine when you saw nobody by this basin: that it was waiting for you?' I was unable to answer. What was it in me that made me rush into danger time and time again? When we washed the next morning I saw the notice above the bowl: 'For *Kapos* only.'

In the following days I began to observe how some of us did not bother to wash properly, merely dabbing at themselves with the freezing water. Others did not even leave the block to wash at all. Myself and Pierre were among those who washed with care and I now wonder whether this early hygenic distinction marked those who might survive and those who almost certainly would not.

We went back to the block, where the *Blockälteste* and his assistants distributed the food, some ersatz coffee and a small piece of bread with a thin sliver of margarine, our ration of solid food for the whole day. There was even a piece of salami on that first morning and I did not realise what a luxury this was. Pierre and I sat on the floor, devoured the bread and salami and gulped down the hot but tasteless coffee.

A small person I recognised from an adjoining bunk came and sat with us. He looked haggard and anxious and began to complain bitterly. 'The man I have to share a bunk with, it's impossible. Have you seen the size of him? I can hardly sleep, I am forced to lie on the frame he is so big. It's terrible. I cannot endure it. He got up to piss and woke me, but what does he care?'

We tried to look sympathetic, but here it was every man for himself and I could only thank my luck that I had Pierre as a sleeping companion.

'Finish and return to your bunks!' the *Blockälteste* announced.

I looked anxiously at Pierre, my face still throbbing from the *Kapo's* fist. 'What can he want?'

'Take it easy,' replied my good friend.

We returned to our bunk and the *Blockälteste's* assistant, who wore a red triangle, appeared. 'Assemble round this bunk, all you new ones here! I am going to show you how your bunk must look every morning! We call this *Bettenbauen* [bed construction].' The *Stubendienst* smoothed out the mattress, folded the blanket neatly and placed it precisely over the thin, straw-filled pillow. When he had finished, the whole assembly was a fanatically neat array of right angles. I looked on in dismay. 'You have five minutes to do this and then I will check your efforts,' the assistant told us. 'I am timing you with my watch.'

Pierre and I returned to our bunk and began. All was chaos at first as six of us collided and cursed as we struggled to make up bunks on three tiers. Eventually we understood that the top bunk should be made first as its owners had to stand on the frame of the middle bunk, mine and Pierre's, to get to it. The *Stubendienst* was not satisfied with any of our efforts and angrily threw the covers back. 'Again!' he ordered. We now agreed it was easier for only three to do this *Bettenbauen*. 'I'll do our bunk,' said Pierre, and I gladly stepped aside. When the *Stubendienst* returned he seemed satisfied, but delivered a stinging slap to the face of some unfortunate by another bunk. Our group of six fell into a bed-making routine. The person in the top bunk would stand on the frame of the middle bed, while those in the bottom bunk made up their bunk at the same time. Pierre then made up our middle bunk.

The *Blockälteste* came and addressed us. 'Now I am going to teach you how you will behave in this camp.' He demonstrated the obligatory ritual of '*Mützen auf*' and '*Mützen ab*' – the putting on and taking off of hats whenever we passed an SS officer. 'You come to attention! You slap your cap smartly against your thigh! If an officer addresses you, you will answer with your number!' I listened in great apprehension to this litany of regulations. 'The reputation of this block depends on you!' continued the *Blockälteste*, 'if I hear any complaints, I will personally discipline you, you can be sure!' I thought of the two truncheons I had seen in the *Tagesraum*.

The *Blockälteste* proved as good as his word. The very next day one of my transport got into an argument with a Polish prisoner in our block. The Polish prisoner, who bore a red triangle, slapped the newcomer's face and the newcomer, a strong and spirited individual, hit him back. A fight developed, and we were trying to pull the antagonists apart when the *Blockälteste* arrived with his truncheon. 'Listen, you Jews! This prisoner,' and he pointed to the Pole, 'works in the administration office. He is one of my assistants in this block! He is responsible for good order here! Therefore he has the right to discipline you. Now I am going to punish this man. Remove your trousers and bend down!' The *Blockälteste* then struck the man hard ten times on his behind with what sounded like the hollow truncheon. He then allowed the man to go to the *Krankenbau*, the camp hospital. Before long the man returned. 'They put some cream on it. I am only bruised and cut,' he told us.

I learnt from this incident not to argue with any inmate who wore either the red triangle of the political prisoner or the green triangle of the German criminal. Older prisoners – that is to say, those with lower numbers – enlightened me as to the meaning of other symbols worn in Auschwitz: the black triangle for the gypsy, the pink for the homosexual, the purple for the church minister and Jehovah's Witness. We Jews only had our Star of David. It was those with red and green triangles who had the privileged positions in the camp, and these were the ones to be feared and courted.

It was on this second day that I was able to take in details of my new surroundings. There were artificial flowers on the walls of the *Tagesraum*, and newspaper clippings. There were six bunks in here, one each for the *Blockälteste's* assistants. Beyond this room was another whose interior I never saw because it was the *Blockälteste's* quarters, where he lived with his *Pipel*, the boy who had led us to our block on the first day. It was not long before I understood the role of these boy assistants, who were a common feature of life in the camp. This *Pipel's* father, a Polish Jew, was in our block. Toughened by long suffering well before the Nazis arrived, the Polish Jews were great organisers and survivors in Auschwitz. But I found the father weeping on his bunk one evening, unable to bear any longer the thought of what was happening to his son. 'The *Blockälteste* ... it was enough having to watch him touch my boy. Now he has taken him...' The only consolation for the father was the extra rations the boy received. The father benefited, too, from his son's portion.

We, the ordinary prisoners – the *Häftlinge* – lived in the other part of the barrack, dominated by rows of packed bunks divided by two corridors. A long table with benches was the only furniture.

The *Blockälteste's* threats of the consequences of failing in any way to come up to standard reverberated in my mind long after his words had ended. Whereas in Paris I had yearned to be the centre of attention, revelling in the cheery camaraderie of the streets of Pigalle, I realised that here invisibility and compliance were my only strategy.

I lined up for the soup that evening, and as I approached the cauldron I saw that the *Blockälteste* had a list in his hand and was calling out a number in response to the number given by the prisoner. 'One five seven one zero three!' I called, and the *Blockälteste* consulted his list. '*Kommando* 95!'

I was very disappointed that Pierre had been assigned to a different work group, *Kommando* 43, but he was his usual smiling self. 'Never mind, Freddie, we will talk about our work tomorrow evening.'

That second night in Auschwitz I discovered that, young as I was, I needed to urinate four or five times. This was because what nourishment we had was mainly liquid. So this first night and every subsequent night was marked by continuous movement as one after another of us was forced to drag his exhausted body from sleep.

Even to this act of nature was appended the Auschwitz ritual of privilege, humiliation and corruption. For the single slop bucket, shared by the whole block – three hundred of us – was overseen by a prisoner given the role of *Nachtwache*, or night guard. He was a Polish Jew called Moishe. All day long he slept in his bunk, and received extra rations, but by night he watched over the bucket, situated just inside the door of the block, for nobody was allowed to leave the building by night without the night guard's permission. The bucket, a very large one, stood on a large sheet which absorbed anything that missed. You pissed and shat under the *Nachtwache's* gaze and he would report any failures of proper aim to the *Blockälteste*, who would punish the miscreant with five blows to the bare backside. The night guard's main duty was to ensure that the bucket did not overflow, while the duty to empty the bucket fell upon the unfortunate individual whose urine or excrement filled it to the top.

This happened to me on several occasions. 'What is your number?' the *Nachtwache* would ask, and I knew it was my fate to empty the huge bucket. He would then make a note of my number. Utterly miserable, I retraced my steps to my bunk and put on my trousers and shirt, as was the rule. Then back to the night guard, who gave me a pair of wooden shoes. For some reason we could not use our own for this duty. The bucket, though at least near the door, was extremely heavy and one had to be careful not to spill a drop. The latrine was not far away, opposite the block, but the weight of the bucket was terrible. Even outside, one tried not to spill anything. Despite all my efforts, I often failed and splashed urine, or worse, on my trousers. Bribery was commonplace. For bread or soup the night guard would pass this exhausting chore to the next individual, but I would rather be condemned to the emptying than give up a crumb of my ration. An older prisoner later told me, 'When I want to piss, I lie awake, waiting for someone else to piss, because I can tell from the sound of the bucket how full it is.' I heeded his advice, and tried to assess the pitch of the sound coming from the bucket. This was easy when the bucket was low in content and gave off a metallic noise, but as it filled my musical training proved inadequate and I could never gauge from the sound the approximate level of the bucket.

Shouts from the *Stubendienst* of '*Raus! Aufstehen!*' ended my sleep. It was to be my first day of work, and I shall never forget it. I ran with Pierre to wash. Others made their bunks first. There was no rule, so long as the bunk was perfectly made. After the coffee and distribution of our daily bread ration of 200 grams, we were assembled in front of the barrack. The *Blockälteste* counted us and then issued orders: '*Kommando* 95! Follow that *Kapo!*' And all those in my *Kommando* followed the *Kapo* to our assigned place on the *Appellplatz*. It was all thoroughly organised. In front of us stood *Kommando 94* and behind us *Kommando 96*. The *Kommando* with the lowest number stood nearest the entrance to the camp. What would my work group have to do? What Pierre's? I was afraid, for until this point I had not realised how much I relied on the fellowship of Pierre, who possessed just that air of calm and competence I lacked. I had only his words to cling to: 'We will discuss our work in the evening.'

The *Kapo* ordered us to move forward and I marched with *Kommando* 95 through the gate I had entered just two days before. Here we were counted again and the *Kapo* called out to the attendant SS men, '*Arbeits Kommando 95 mit 154 Häftlinge zur Arbeit!* Work group 95 with 154 prisoners to work!' The *Kapo* shouted *Mützen ab!* and as we passed the SS we removed our caps in the prescribed manner as the camp orchestra played us out to our new place of work. I felt strangely exposed without the familiar feel of my glasses on the end of my nose, but their absence was no great practical hindrance because there was nothing to read in Auschwitz, save the motto over the entrance.

After about thirty minutes of awkward marching in our wooden shoes, which rubbed my skin painfully, my *Kommando* arrived at an unfinished factory complex. Inmates from other

173

work groups, lower-number ones who had therefore left the camp before us, were already busy, digging, carrying metal bars, hauling railway wagons. They all seemed to be working with maximum effort. There were also German civilians with the title '*Meister*', who had expertise in specific fields and acted as heads of works, overseeing operations. They had nothing to do with discipline, but would report any problem to the SS. They soon moved on to other tasks.

Our *Kapo* led us to a line of railway wagons, around which many prisoners were gathered. Men on the wagons were lifting sacks of cement, each weighing twenty-five kilograms, on to the shoulders of prisoners below, while others were shovelling cement into wheelbarrows, which were then trundled away towards one of the many buildings under construction.

My heart sank as the reality of *Kommando* 95 was revealed: hard physical labour on undernourished stomachs. Into my mind came a film I had seen in Vienna about the slaves in Egypt. There the slaves were struck with whips to encourage their efforts; here the *Kapos* yelled '*Faster!*' and used sticks. Our *Kapo* ordered two of our group on to the wagon and two others into the building on the double. 'You in the building, when the cement arrives, open the bags and make a pile of it. The remainder of you *Franzosen*, you carry the bags to that building.' The *Kapo* pointed to a building some 150 metres away. '*Franzosen*': it was what the *Blockältaeste* had called all of us in Block 53. It reinforced the Nazi thinking, that we had no identity in their eyes save the number on our arm. They had taken away our hair, to reduce our physical distinctiveness. And now they were eradicating our history, the thing that defines the identity of every human being. German, Austrian, French, Dutch – it made no difference. We were

Franzosen, Frenchmen, because we had all come from Drancy. That small past was all they allowed us.

I had little time to dwell on such thoughts because now one of the prisoners on the truck lowered a bag of cement on my back and I staggered under its crushing weight towards the building. I dumped this first bag, paused to catch my breath, but to shouts of '*Schnell!*' from the *Kapo* I half ran, half walked back for the next. With each successive journey the bag became heavier and the distance between truck and building greater. I had no eyes for anybody else in that chain of remorseless labour. Besides, we were forbidden to talk to one another. Every so often an SS officer would approach and the *Kapo*, anxious to retain his privileged status, would use his stick on any unfortunate *Häftling* within range, urging him to work harder with shouts of '*Los! Schnell!*' Rest was forbidden. The only way to gain brief respite was to ask permission from the *Kapo* to use the latrine, and even this was allowed only twice a day, once in the morning and once in the afternoon. The *Kapo* would give the easy job of supervising the latrine to one of his favourite underlings. This person, usually an experienced prisoner, was known as the Scheissmeister, or shit supervisor. He ensured that we did not linger long in the latrine. Other privileged prisoners also supervised us – usually those with red triangles, or other favourites who hung around with the *Kapo*.

I had devoured the morning's bread ration as soon as I got it into my hands. As I toiled in the cold, all I thought of apart from the next bag of cement was the midday soup. In Auschwitz I learnt that you never get used to hunger. All I ever wanted there was food.

The builders of the Buna factory complex were not prisoners as such. Some workers were German civilians, some were Poles and there were other conscripted labourers, mainly from France. They were paid for their labour. More importantly, they had decent food. We were forbidden to speak to them, and they to us, but I tried. I would do almost anything for food, or a cigarette to barter for food. I sometimes approached the French labourers, hoping for some advantage because I spoke their language. They ignored me, or looked about themselves nervously, fearful of the SS. Rarely did I gain anything.

Finally, the siren from the Buna factory howled the end of the morning's work. I went to the soup barrel, hoping to find some vegetables in the soup, but no, the liquid was so thin that no matter how deeply the *Kapo* plunged his ladle, I could still see its shape quite clearly. I drank deeply and, aching all over, threw myself down in exhaustion to sleep, only to sleep, for as long as possible, although only half an hour was given to us. It seemed that no sooner had I closed my eyes than the *Kapos'* shouts and blasts of their whistle dragged me back to consciousness. Once again I carried bags of cement from train to building. Later, I heard the siren at Buna, calling the German workers from their lunch break, and it felt like mockery to me, who had already been labouring for a whole hour.

There was one person in our group who had been on the same transport as me from Drancy, which I knew because of his number. He was a real Frenchman, called Marcel, one of those rare, inexplicable characters who seemed untouched by the world of the camp. He was about twenty years old and had been a weightlifter. His broad shoulders bore witness to this, and the ease with which he carried a cement bag was matched by his cheerful expression. Whenever I passed him to collect another bag, he sang quietly, '*Courage, camarades! On les aura!* Come on, comrades! We'll beat them!' We all sought to be within his orbit.

I, who considered myself an eternal optimist, could only seek to follow his example and encourage fellow prisoners whenever possible. Pierre and I liked to talk to him. '*Courage!*' he would say again, whenever we heard rumours of the Allied advance. Just hearing Marcel warmed my heart with hope. This spirit of his did not seem the unthinking hopefulness of a fool, but something arising from a deep part of himself which genuinely believed in the triumph of goodness over evil. Knowing Marcel was a humbling experience, but although he did not sleep far from us I do not know whether he survived Auschwitz.

The *Kapo*'s whistle sounded the end of the day's work. I had never known such exhaustion and felt certain that the Cement *Kommando* would be the end of me. Those around me looked equally fatigued.

Now we marched for about half an hour, in an absurd parody of soldiers, back to the camp. I saw the gate and heard the music, some march or other. I glanced up at the inscription and thought, yes, work will free us, it will kill us and then we will be free. Then I looked towards the orchestra and saw that there were only two cellos in it, and an idea formed in my impulsive head. If only I could only get myself into the orchestra. The *Kapo* shouted, '*Mützen ab!*' and 154 exhausted souls snapped their caps from their heads and passed into the camp as the *Kapo* announced the return of our full complement to the waiting SS men: '*Arbeits Kommando 95 mit 154 Häftlinge zurück im Lager!*'

At last, the evening gruel. 'It's thicker in the evening,' an older prisoner had told me. Yet it took me days to learn the important trick, to contrive not to be among the first served. That way one was more likely to get some of the meagre portion of vegetables nestling at the bottom of the pot.

177

I made it my business to try to befriend the 'Prominents', the privileged prisoners, in our block. I was not often successful, but there was one, a Czech political prisoner called Janek, who spoke perfect German. As most of the people in our block were French I went out of my way to speak to him in German on whatever pretext was to hand. He seemed to like me and Pierre and we often spoke to him of political matters. Both he and Pierre were confirmed communists and spoke eloquently of the just society of communism, which would surely arise out of the ashes of this fascist nightmare. Janek was certain that the Russians would dominate the world and bring such a society to pass, but his voice softened as he spoke about his girlfriend, who was waiting for him in a little village in his country. Importantly, Janek quite often distributed the soup. He would dig deeper with his ladle, to procure a few vegetables for me or Pierre and give us a larger ration of bread than we usually received.

I was astonished when I met my bunk partner after our first day's work, because he seemed in a much better state than me. 'How is this, Pierre? I am dead, the whole day carrying bags of cement. My feet are so sore. What have you been doing?'

'You know, I am on the Locksmith *Kommando*, it's not such a hard number.'

I was astonished. 'How did you manage this?' I asked.

'Oh, you know,' he answered with his normal insouciance, 'when we registered and they asked me if I had a trade or profession, I said I had been a locksmith. I did work with one in Marseilles for a while.' He grinned at me.

Later, when I thought about this turn of events, I was not really so surprised at Pierre's aplomb. Someone like him would instinctively understand that when you were asked a question you placed yourself in the best possible light, especially when your answer could never be verified. Still, I cursed myself for the unthinking and naive fool I was, a man who had declared that he was a student.

I was determined to rescue myself from the serious position I had fallen into, and my thoughts returned to the orchestra.

We were allowed to drift around after work within the confines of the camp from the end of the day's work until ordered to our bunks. As soon as I had drank to the very bottom of my *Schüssel* I found out that the Musicians' Block, number 33, was by the entrance to the camp, near where they played each day. As I made my way through the complex of blocks I was sure that all my worries would be over. I already saw myself, sitting with my cello, playing rather than slowly dying. I felt elated that I had studied the cello. How extraordinary, what a stroke of luck, I told myself, that this boyhood accomplishment might save me from the hard labour of the Cement *Kommando*! I approached Block 33 wild with optimism, knocked on the door and smiled ingratiatingly at the middle-aged Jewish prisoner who opened it and gazed at me questioningly. I explained that I was a cellist. He looked at me and almost laughed. 'How old are you? Sixteen or seventeen? We do not have amateurs here.' I persisted and he told me to wait a minute. A few moments later he returned with a man I recognised as the conductor, another middle-aged man, rather tall, and a political prisoner from Poland. I explained that I had studied the cello since I was six. 'And now I am twenty-two,' I said, pleading with him, 'so I have played for many years, you know.'

The conductor looked at me sympathetically. He knew why I was there, what I sought to escape from. 'Tell me about your experiences with orchestras,' he asked.

Haltingly, I told him that I had played in my school orchestra,

179

and with my brothers in a trio: light pieces, for entertainment, at charities and suchlike. There was no point in lying, I would be found out.

The conductor shook his head sadly. 'Look, the musicians in this orchestra are professionals. We have professors of music academies here. I cannot take on amateurs, I really can't. I am sorry.' He wished me luck and sent me on my way.

I was deeply disappointed, my dream of a different, easier life in this hell in shreds. It seemed that perpetual hunger and crippling work were to remain my lot.

It was then that I had a remarkable stroke of luck. As I wandered back to my barrack I saw the familiar figure of Professor Waitz. I called out and rushed over to him. He looked at me and greeted me warmly. 'Freddie, it's so good to see you! What has been happening to you here?'

I wasted no time pouring out my woes. We spoke in French, as I did even with Pierre – because we rejected our Austrian background, though when we spoke we did drop in a few Viennese slang words – 'If only I had thought to tell them I had a trade…' I said, 'and then I tried for the orchestra just now but they rejected me outright. The Cement *Kommando*… I think I will die of exhaustion here. I have made a friend, we share a bunk, he is on the Locksmith *Kommando* and is happy there.'

'Listen to me, Freddie. You were kind to me on the train. I have a good job here, working in the hospital. You come to me any evening you can, and I will try to get you some extra food. As for your job, I will see what I can do.'

I thanked Professor Waitz from the bottom of my heart and when I left him I felt that my luck had not deserted me after all. I believed there was a good chance that I would survive this ordeal, so that I could tell the world what the Nazis had done to the Jews.

I told Pierre my news, the good and the bad.

'If this professor is as fine a man as he seems, he will do something for you.'

'If only I could get on to your *Kommando*, Pierre.'

Professor Waitz proved as good as his word. Every evening I was able to, I crossed to the hospital, by the eastern perimeter of the camp. Although he was often busy treating people, the Professor would smile and gesture to me to take some soup and bread. As a Prominent, he always had a good ration of food.

So it was that my friendship with Professor Waitz saved my life. I was one of the fortunate ones. Very occasionally I would bring back a piece of bread for Pierre, and in this way repaid him for his guardianship of me and for the fact that every morning it was he who loyally continued to make up our bunk.

But I was not yet free of the Cement *Kommando*. Sustained by the extra rations I was able at least to endure the crushing weight of the bags, but no extra rations could prevent my body from aching nor relieve my fear of the rubber truncheon if I did not work as fast as they demanded. All day, every day, I longed only for food and sleep.

My feet rapidly blistered under the tremendous weight of the cement. I felt as if they were exploding under the pressure from above as the stiff canvas lining of my shoes rubbed remorselessly against unprotected skin. I went to visit the Professor. He looked grave as he examined my feet. 'None too soon, Freddie,' he said. 'This can become a dangerous condition, incurable in fact.' He looked at me meaningfully as he added, 'people with *dicke Füsse*, swollen feet, are not seen again. Take this cream...'

It was Janek who told me about the machine grease inmates used to rub into the canvas of their shoes. 'Yes, you can get it from the *Blockälteste*. It gets smuggled in.' As it was the duty of the *Blockälteste* to ensure that the prisoners in his charge were fit enough to work, he would distribute this grease when he could get it. In this way I was able to relieve some of the suffering.

My luck improved in another way, too, for after a few days I was moved to the wheelbarrows and so my work became a little lighter. Nevertheless, there are two particular days on the Cement *Kommando* which stand out in my mind.

On one of those days it was raining as I lined up with my *Kommando* as usual in the *Appellplatz*. The thought of carrying the bags, made even heavier by rain, filled me with foreboding, but at the Buna factory a pleasant surprise awaited me. The *Kapo* informed us that the cement had not arrived. 'Today you will dig roads,' he said. My heart lifted as we were divided into groups of ten and given shovels and told to get on with it by the *Kapo's* underling, who promptly disappeared into his hut. This man was a Frenchman and a communist, who hated the Nazis and so left us to our own devices.

Unsupervised, we were even able to talk to one another, while keeping our eyes open for SS or less sympathetic *Kapos*. But what do Frenchmen, real Frenchmen, not the *Franzosen* the *Kapos* still called all of us, talk about? Food! Wine, garlic and pâté predominated. Each Frenchman conjured up the specialities of his region. 'Freddie, what would you cook?' I was eventually asked. I had to admit that I had never cooked in my life, so instead I offered them my food fantasy. It went like this: I had been liberated, and returned to my little apartment in Pigalle. I enter my kitchenette and fill a big aluminium bucket to the brim with melted chocolate and set the bucket, along with a quantity of biscuits, on the floor by my sofa bed. I lie back on the sofa, turn on the radio, which is either playing Dvořák's *New World Symphony* or Gershwin's *Rhapsody in Blue*. I have a china cup which I repeatedly fill with the chocolate until the bucket is drained. I then finish the plate of biscuits and just lie there as the music wafts from the radio, imagining myself playing my cello in the orchestra. My naive dream created much laughter, but my stomach did not enjoy all this talk about food. I had only told them my dream in the first place just to keep in with the general mood. The *Kapo's* underling had joined our group and seemed to enjoy listening to our stories, but he got us back to work whenever an SS man approached.

When the siren howled I ran to the hut, where the thin, hot soup awaited us. Then this small idyll came to an abrupt end. 'The cement has arrived,' the *Kapo* informed us, and with sinking heart I looked forward to a long, hard afternoon.

The other memorable event during my time on the Cement *Kommando* was an unpleasant one. It was the second occasion on which I was personally subjected to violence. As usual it was my impulsiveness which was the cause.

Everyone knew that there were British POWs at Auschwitz, and these prisoners had a reputation for friendliness towards the *Häftlinge*. They worked in the factory under an entirely different regime to ours, well clothed and in receipt of regular Red Cross parcels. One man in our block had shown us two cigarettes he had got from a British POW.

On this particular day I saw a group of British prisoners working not too far away from us. I asked the *Kapo* for permission to use the latrine but instead ambled towards the

POWs, who were not divided from us by any fence or barbed wire. How warm they looked in their wool-lined jackets! I asked them for a cigarette and one of them threw a half-smoked one towards me. A cigarette was a valuable commodity, and a small one that could easily be hidden. I put the cigarette in my trouser pocket and turned back, convinced I had got away with it. Then I heard a sound and saw our *Kapo* running over to me. He struck me full in the face. Once again blood streamed and the *Kapo* dragged me to his hut, where he pulled the cigarette from my pocket. He took his rubber truncheon. 'Lower your trousers,' he ordered. I did so and he gave me ten hard blows on my backside. The pain was dreadful, but I managed to remain silent under this punishment until I returned to the piled bags of cement, where I gave in to weeping. The parting words of the *Kapo* echoed in my head: 'You were lucky you didn't get the full twenty-five, but I am in a good mood today.'

The *Kapo* did not discover the cement bag I had taken from an outbuilding as some protection against the biting cold and placed under my shirt. I would have been severely punished if it had been discovered, but it was worth the risk because it really provided excellent insulation. From time to time I replaced it with a newer bag.

Professor Waitz organised my transfer. One evening, after I had been in Auschwitz about two weeks, I was eating my soup with Pierre. The *Blockälteste* was assigning certain members of my block to the hospital when he called my number: 'One five seven one zero three! You are now in *Kommando* 43! Line up with that *Kommando* tomorrow morning.' I turned to Pierre, overjoyed. 'Now we will work together!' he said, as happy as I was. He wasted no time telling me about his *Kommando*. 'You won't have any trouble with the *Kapo*. Even the German *Meister*, and he's a real Nazi with his party badge, though he is curt with us, is not abusive.' And later he promised me, 'I will teach you how to steal from there.'

When I went to collect my extra rations the next time, I thanked the Professor with all my heart. He put his arm around my and said, 'You are a friend, Freddie, a friend.' Such acts of fellowship reminded me that I was still a human being.

Yet even the life of a Prominent could come to an end violently. It was the spring of 1944, and I had been working on the Locksmith *Kommando* for a year or so, when one evening we marched wearily through the clogging Polish soil from our place of work, the wooden shoes hurting our feet despite the use of the machine grease. At least, with my cement bag, I had some protection from the elements. As usual, the camp orchestra, which was no more than a sound to me now, played on and our *Kapo* announced that he had his full complement to the SS men. The routine was unchanging, but today, instead of being marched to our block, we were directed to the *Appellplatz* and ordered to line up.

In the gathering dusk the powerful beam of the watchtower illuminated three black gallows set up on a platform. Three vacant chairs beneath the gallows awaited the victims. It was like a stage set and soon enough the players appeared, first SS men with machine guns, who took up positions on the perimeter, then SS *Hauptsturmführer* Schwarz with his entourage of officers.[1] The *Kapo*s shouted, '*Mützen ab!*' and fifteen thousand exhausted prisoners removed their wet rags from their heads. The *Lagerälteste* marched with three SS men to a nearby bunker and brought out three men, their hands tied behind their backs. When the light caught their pale faces, I recognised them at once. They were

185

three Prominents, envied by all of us because they worked in the SS barracks, which gave them access to better food. Three *Kapos* now led the three men, all of whom I saw bore a fixed and defiant demeanour, to the gallows. The SS had their machine guns trained on us. The *Kapos* put the noose around the prisoners' necks and pushed them up on to the chairs. An officer now addressed us in loud, bombastic words. 'In the name of the German people and by order of SS *Reichsführer* Himmler the three prisoners, Nathan Weissmann, Janek Grossfeld and Leo Diament, are condemned to death by hanging for their treacherous activities against the German Reich!' We were not told the nature of these activities, but hearing a prisoner, one of us, addressed by name by the Germans was a strange experience.

There was a short silence and then a single thin, clear voice called out from the gallows, '*Kopf hoch, Kamaraden, wir sind die Letzten*. Have courage, comrades, we are the last ones.' Then came a shout from another of the condemned: '*Es lebe die Freiheit!* Long live freedom!' Some small spark of life returned to me with these bold words, which lifted me to that higher vision of mankind I had all but forgotten in the small, dark world of self-preservation in which I was forced to live. The officer became enraged because he and his fellow tormentors had suffered a moral defeat. '*Los!* Get on with it!' he shouted, and the three *Kapos* kicked the chairs away. This loss of composure encouraged all of us, and, as if with one accord, we all called out '*Servus!*', which is both a greeting and a farewell. Our action was greeted with looks of uncertainty from our tormentors. They did not seem to know what to do, and my spirits surged because I could sense their powerlessness against so many of us. But this lofty moment quickly passed and we were marched away to our blocks. But the glow of that instant of defiance and unanimity among us remained and Pierre and I spoke of it together warmly: how the Germans had miscalculated our reaction to their horrible show executions, how bravely those who had perished on the gallows had defied their enemy, as we must do.

Yet in the end we each separated back into our individual existences. All that mattered to me was that I was alive. I could think no further than the next bowl of soup and the friendship that Pierre provided. And even we, as we lay head to foot in our bunks, were torment to each other. It was the smell of our feet, particularly mine. They stank from the suppurations caused by the wooden shoes, and there was little one could do about it. Rumours circulated that the three hanged men had been involved in some form of collusion with the *Schreibstube*, the administration office, or a *Blockälteste*, with the aim of saving people from the Selections. Nobody knew, nobody could be sure, few had enough energy to care.

For it was enough to get through the next Selection. The Polish prisoners, who always seemed to get wind of one first, ran around calling out '*Selectja! Selectja!*' I approached each Selection with nothing but a grim determination to survive.

I passed my very first Selection one Sunday just after I joined the Locksmith *Kommando*. 'You will remain in the block!' announced the *Blockälteste*. It was always on a Sunday, always those words, so we knew the Poles had been right. 'Go to your bunks! Strip naked!' he ordered. And we waited for the arrival of the Germans. Pierre and I stood side by side, bolstering each other with encouragement and advice. Do I not look healthy? Of course you do. Strong enough for more manual labour? Certainly! Just throw your chest out as you go in front of them, walk with confidence and a resolute expression. That's what impresses them. But do I look like a *Muselmann*? Are you crazy? Just look at them.

'*Muselmann*' was the name we gave the doomed. They were all around us. Which of them would go up the chimney this time? Of course we were all bags of bones, but the *Muselmann* was terrible to behold. It was not just his yellow pallor which marked him out. The *Muselmann* was hunched, meek, resigned and moved only with effort. There were often tears in his eyes. I averted my eyes from such prisoners because even a glance from one of them might infect me. All I could feel for them was a contemptuous pity. Sympathy was a sentiment from another, lost world. Sometimes the *Blockälteste* would not need to wait for the judgement of an SS doctor, but would separate a *Muselmann* or two from the rest us before his arrival. To allow such individuals, for whom liquidation was an inevitability, to waste the time of the SS would have reflected badly on him.

'You have nothing to fear! You have a lot of strength and spirit in you...!' But our words counted for nothing now, for the SS had arrived, one of them a doctor in a white coat. They took their places in the Tagesraum with the *Blockälteste*. We naked *Häftlinge* lined up in front of the entrance. In front of me human being after human being, so many units of work to the Germans, called out their number as they moved forward to their judges. The SS ordered each man to turn around and then the doctor gazed briefly at what appeared to be his behind, before dismissing him. Why was this? Yes, I soon knew that fleshless, flat buttocks was a sure sign that a man had outlived his usefulness, was a Muselmann. At the sight of such buttocks the SS doctor's hand would probably note the number of the owner of the buttocks.

'*One five seven one zero three!*' I shouted my number, marching before their impassive faces with head held high in an absurd parody of confidence. Turn round now, one of them said, and they looked at my buttocks. A pause, the pause of cool assessment. Should I live or die? And then they let me go. Had I passed? I did not know, but after a day had gone by and nothing had happened I knew I was safe this time. I thanked my luck. I thanked the extra rations I got through Professor Waitz, which put the requisite flesh on my buttocks.

I don't know how many Selections I went through. Perhaps it is only the first that I remember, perhaps they have all merged into one, a repeating nightmare which changes only in minor detail. But with each the insignificance of my existence or non-existence in the eyes of the Germans was confirmed anew and I therefore clung to life with opposing stubbornness. To the reader it may seem that I mention little of the changing seasons, but for me, Auschwitz had no seasons. If it was ever warm, I don't remember it. I lived without awareness of anything save hunger, work and the Selections.

I began to steal from my fellow prisoners, who dwelt, like me, on the edge of extinction. In so doing I violated all bonds of human trust and kinship, and it was always, always for food that I did it.

Not long after I arrived at the camp I observed a man on my own *Kommando* eat only half his bread. He must have thought that nobody saw him hide the other half under the straw mattress of his bunk, probably to eat when he returned from work. I did not think to take this man's bread, almost his sole source of nourishment, but when we returned from work he was howling as he rifled desperately through his bunk. I will never forget the look on his face. Yet, later, I likewise stole. I remember my victim,

189

a poor Hungarian, but I cared nothing for his anguish. So far as I was concerned, I had struck lucky. I had long contrived to linger a little longer in the block so as to carry out such searches for hidden food.

One day I was standing to attention in my *Kommando*, about to march out to work, when an incident in another waiting *Kommando* drew my gaze. A *Kapo* had struck a prisoner. I recognised the prisoner as Bernie, whom I had not seen since we left Drancy. I saw him again one evening in the hour between the soup and going to our bunks. We spoke without emotion. We were just two shaved, starved prisoners. 'They hit me because I was not standing properly to attention. It's a pity we did not finish that tunnel. There's no escape from this place.' I did not see Bernie again.

The *Kapo* on my new *Kommando* was a green-triangle prisoner, but he seemed altogether a milder character than the *Kapo* from the Cement *Kommando*, just as Pierre had told me. We had been taken to a building and given the job of moving heavy pieces of metal from one place to another. The *Kapo* prepared a fire in a metal drum. This work was paradise compared with working outside. After dumping the metal pieces I had the joy of passing the glowing flames of the fire. We could warm our hands in its heat for a few seconds, testing the *Kapo's* tolerance to the point where he would stir himself and chase us away.

Pierre had taken me in on his stealing activities and demonstrated his smuggling system. This we were able to accomplish only when detailed to some remote part of the building. 'Freddie, look and learn. You make a bundle like this…' he said, wrapping up a few nails in a piece of cloth. Next he took a piece of wire and tied it to the bundle, then slid the assembly down his trouser

190

leg to knee height and tied the other end of the wire to his waist. The penalty for being caught was twenty-five strokes on the backside if a *Kapo* caught you, almost certain death if the SS did. Once Pierre even managed to steal a small hammer, tying it to his back with a piece of string. We would take our pickings to the *Kapo*s. For ten nails, one bowl of soup. In bundles of old cloth we smuggled machine grease for use on shoes into the camp. If our *Blockälteste* had his supply of grease, or anything else we brought in, we would try to peddle our loot in another barrack. In this way we survived.

Around May 1944, about six months after I arrived at Auschwitz, the Nazis staged another display. In the camp was a French Jewish boxer called Victor Perez, who had once been world flyweight champion. I often spoke to him, though his speech was slurred and his wits slow from all the blows he had taken in the ring. As a boxer he had a privileged position in the kitchens, so his handicapped brain was no real disadvantage to him in Auschwitz. He was from Tunis, he told me. 'I was arrested in Paris, in Belleville,' he said. It turned out that we had been on the same transport from Drancy. He seemed to have good relations with all around him. I think that even the SS admired him for his sporting past.

Sometime that summer news spread that Perez and others were going to fight in the camp. Sure enough, a boxing ring was constructed in the *Appellplatz*. There were seats all around the ring for the SS and other officials. We knew the event was to take place on a Sunday, after our evening soup. Pierre and I wandered over to the *Appellplatz*. Seated on one side of the ring were about two hundred SS men of various ranks, some of whom, we heard, had come from surrounding satellite camps.

191

On the other side sat the *Lagerälteste* and other Prominents. Pierre and I stood behind the Prominents to watch the fights. Perez climbed into the ring, warmed up with a skipping rope and did some shadow boxing. His opponent, a much bigger man, entered the ring. The referee, an SS man, announced that this man was a boxer in the Wehrmacht. The fight lasted just three rounds, with Perez avoiding blows and landing a few on his opponent. At the end the referee declared the contest a draw. Perez would never have dared inflict real injury on his opponent and his opponent probably knew that, if he tried to do the same, Perez would have more than defended himself as his boxing instincts prevailed.[2]

It was in June 1944 that the Hungarian Jews arrived, in convoy after convoy. They flooded every block, filling the places left by the ones who had disappeared. Nobody could speak their outlandish tongue and their German, if they had it, was so accented it was almost impossible to understand. A few came to our block, including the one whose food I stole. There was one of their number who did speak good German. His name was Imre, a tall, skinny fellow, and he came from Budapest.[3] I told him about my holidays in Lake Balaton. 'Look, I can sing a Hungarian children's song, about the sound of locomotives!' I told him, and did so. Phonetically, this is what I sang for Imre, this innocent, onomatopoeic rhyme: *'Ozem Roszam Voshutosh, Voshutosh, Hotch a nemshock Osutosh, Miindiar Megeloel...'*

He laughed, even complimenting me on my accent. I didn't mention it to him, but this was a song I had learnt from pretty Rosza, the girl with whom I had fallen in love when I was fourteen. I was twenty-three now, so it had been only nine years ago, but that span of time seemed an eternity.

Imre talked about Hungary. 'A country of peasants and workers, but some are academics, like me. I was at the University...' He must have told me what he did there, but I cannot remember. 'I was arrested with my wife, and my young daughter,' he told me. 'If only I can find out which camp the Nazis have put them.' I lowered my eyes before such naivety. I told him to forget about them, and he looked at me in horror. But I went on anyway. 'Forget being a gentleman here. If you want to survive you'll have to organise extra food, you won't live on what they give you here. Steal it or make friends in high places. Believe me, that is life here. Survival, nothing more, and to survive you must eat.' I could see that Imre did not believe me. It was impossible for him to adapt his view of the world to Auschwitz. I could see him shy away from me in disgust. I was an animal in his eyes. He never spoke to me again. I saw him a few weeks later and he bore the mark of a *Muselmann*.

One day that summer we had returned from our labouring, as tired as ever, and came upon a strange sight. An excited group of *Häftlinge* were standing around a notice pinned to the wall. What could this be? What reason could they possibly have to communicate with us in this manner? We, who were no better than slaves? We drew nearer. Finally I managed to read the notice. It purported to be a concession to us. Every prisoner, it proclaimed, was to be permitted to write a letter to their families. There were several conditions: the letter must be in German and could be sent only to an occupied country, to Germany or to a country allied to Germany. One could not ask for food parcels, but was permitted to thank the recipient for food parcels or letters received. The letter must be written on a special form, available from the *Blockälteste*.

Some seemed taken in by this offer, unable to resist the chance to communicate with their families. Their eyes shone as they spoke animatedly among themselves. For the smallest moment I, too, had been taken in, but this callous propaganda ruse was quickly as clear to me as it was to Pierre, who stood stony-faced beside me. Perhaps this was because we were from Vienna. We had witnessed the behaviour of the Nazis after the Anschluss and tried not to even contemplate the situation of our families now. We were sure that our parents were no longer in Vienna, wherever they were. Besides, I remembered what Tadek had said on my first day in the camp: 'Do you see any old people here?' But some of these others, from occupied countries, still retained hope, were still willing, even eager, to believe. 'Come on!' I said. 'Are you all crazy? Who among you has ever received a food parcel?' Pierre now joined in, shouting, 'What do you imagine this is all about? Think! The Nazis are going to show these letters to the Red Cross, and to the newspapers, to demonstrate how well the Jews here are being treated!' There were mingled sounds of disagreement and softer ones of dismay. One prisoner came up with an idea for a letter. 'I'll send one to a Christian family who know my family. I will word it cleverly, so that they will know the truth. It's worth a try...'

The Allies are in Normandy!' The camp grapevine followed the progress of the war avidly. Then came the news that the Russians had entered Poland. Soon we began to hear artillery and knew our liberators were approaching. The more we heard artillery the happier we were, but we wondered what they would do with us. 'They'll kill us all,' said some. 'They don't want the Russians finding us,' I argued. 'There are too many of us. They will evacuate us.' This proved correct.

Yet none of us knew the full truth of Auschwitz. Our comrades disappeared and we knew they had perished. There was the sickly smell from the crematorium to remind us that people died routinely, but none of us understood the sheer scale of the slaughter. Birkenau, where the gassings were carried out, was an entirely separate camp. Nobody had any notion that Birkenau was a factory of mechanised mass killing.

And then, one beautiful day in August 1944, a Sunday, the allies left their first calling card. We did not work on Sundays. We just hung around in groups, but the sound I heard on that morning was a familiar one at an unfamiliar time: the siren at Buna. We then saw SS men running. We were all nonplussed until the skies filled with the black shapes of aeroplanes. We returned to our blocks but the mood was jubilant. We laughed to think that our liberators were coming. How happy I was to see the Germans run for their lives! I was not afraid to die, nor were those around me. Death was our daily companion. Those who inflicted death, they were the ones afraid to die. The sound of bombs raining down was music to our ears. It was the Buna factory they were targeting. Not one bomb dropped on our blocks, although we were only five kilometres from Buna.

People worked in the factory on Sunday and my joy was muted when some of our number returned from there carrying dead and wounded prisoners. But when one survivor informed us that the factory had been almost completely destroyed and that some SS men and overseers had been killed, I felt only delight. The *Kapo*s redoubled their ferocity, to crush any spirit emerging in us. We spent many days after this air raid clearing up the debris. I was one of many clearing masonry from the roads so that rebuilding of the destroyed parts of the factory could begin. Everyone had to work on this, so that Buna could be rebuilt and the production of artificial rubber resume.

I found a quite recent German newspaper in a waste bin and hid it under my shirt. Never before had I experienced the written word as I did then. It didn't matter that it was mostly propaganda reports of German victories over the Russian savages. We devoured it, because the written word reminded us that we were human, with the power to think, to reflect, to understand a narrative, and to distinguish truth from lies. And although we rejoiced at the reports of the death of German civilians under Allied bombing – '*un autre Boche qui est mort*. Another dead German,' we would say, laughing – we were drawn like the thirsty to water by the accounts of everyday trivia, reminding us that somewhere normality still existed.

The sights and sounds around us told me the truth hidden by the newspaper. At night, when the camp was silent, the boom of artillery, ever louder, made it clear that the days of our imprisonment were nearly over. And then a sound and a sight together: one day, when we were clearing rubble at Buna, we heard youthful voices singing Nazi songs. Looking up, I saw youths, Hitler Youths, drilling and training with rifles under the command of SS men. Some of the boys were raising a Nazi flag on a building. The Germans had been reduced to throwing school children against the Russian artillery. They took these boys on a tour – of us. They wanted them to see the wretched subhuman Jews, dirty, ragged, enemies of the Reich. The Hitler Youths looked at us with loathing. They knew we were their enemy. Had they not been taught: '*Die Juden sind unser Unglück*. The Jews are our misfortune'?

On the night of 17 January 1945 the *Blockälteste* told us that we were leaving the camp. Somehow word got out that the people in the hospital would not be coming with us. 'They will kill them,' prisoners said.

'Where do you think they're taking us?' I asked Pierre.

'I don't know, but surely it will be on foot – the railways must have been destroyed by the bombing.'

That last night in Auschwitz was bitterly cold. I could not sleep for the possibilities which plagued me, possibilities of death on the one hand, and escape and liberation on the other.

The next morning we received extra rations of bread and soup, and were lined up, huddling under the blankets we were permitted to take but still shivering in our striped uniform. I stood with Pierre, while warmly clothed SS men guarded us. It was snowing. I was grateful for my cement bag.

One of an endless column of ragged humanity, I marched into unknown territory.

8

DEATH MARCH

WE STARTED to toil through thick snow, the SS at our flanks. I looked back at the familiar sign presiding over the abandoned camp: '*Arbeit Macht Frei.*' The sound of the artillery, the sound of our liberation, drew ever closer and yet we were drawing away from it with every step. 'How long will we have to march?' I whispered to Pierre. 'Think of nothing except the next step, you should know that by now,' he replied. Soon enough we passed Buna itself, a black, empty monument to Nazi enterprise.

When we reached the country road, walking became even harder because the surface was frozen. It started snowing and icy winds whipped our face while clumps of mud-stained snow dragged at our feet. A prisoner in the column ahead of mine slipped and fell, and seemed unable to get up. An SS man at once dispatched him with a bullet through the head and some prisoners were ordered to throw the body into a ditch.

Now the road ran through a forest. Flight seemed possible. I saw us fleeing, zigzagging to avoid the bullets. I whispered something to Pierre about running, and he said to wait until nightfall. He and I were in a better condition than many others. I had survived because of the vital extra food provided by the Professor, and Pierre's trading activities meant that he was also in better shape than many around us.

Close by I saw another prisoner having difficulty marching. He went to the edge of the road, where there was a pile of stones, and sat down to adjust his shoes; perhaps he wanted to tighten the strings. An SS man ran over and shot him. This time there was no order to throw the body into the ditch because it was so near where the man lay that it was an easy matter for the SS man to kick him into it. The sharp crack of bullets through the freezing air became commonplace. Others supported struggling comrades. I supported nobody. One must keep on one's own feet, I decided; two could slip as easily as one.

We came upon empty villages abandoned before the Russian advance, and all the while the distant rumbling artillery of their heavy guns accompanied us. We dragged ourselves like automatons through one after another of these villages, each seeming to hold out a slender hope that we might be permitted to stop, perhaps even get a little nourishment. A time came when I felt wetness and pain in my foot from the rubbing of the wooden shoes. 'Just keep on your feet,' I again told myself. As it got darker two young men broke from the column and ran for the shadows of the forest. A crack of bullets, and they fell. Pierre murmured that to flee was hopeless.

As night fell we halted at last, and were separated into abandoned barns. Having found a piece of dry earth, I collapsed. I dreamt that I was home again in Vienna with my family, but no sooner had the dream begun than I was dragged from sleep by shouts of 'Raus! Raus! Aufstehen!'

It was dark outside when we assembled, if that is the right word for the shambling, feeble creatures we were. Again the freezing cold, the columns of ten, the rows of five. But where was Pierre? I looked around in panic for him, but he was nowhere to be seen, neither in front nor behind. With his disappearance I felt my one human connection taken from me, almost a part of my history, because Pierre had been beside me since my time in Drancy, but I did not allow myself to dwell on my loss. There were other imperatives to attend to. I had taken no nourishment since leaving Buna and now, all around me, people were stooping to grab up handfuls of snow to slake their raging thirsts. I followed suit, but I did not really believe I could endure another day of this march. I kept marching simply not to be shot. I had no soul, only an instinct to survive. The crack of rifle shots continued, clear, brittle and sharp on the icy air. The artillery in the distance, belonging to those who would come, conquer and perhaps judge, provided the ponderous counterpoint.

A man whose presence beside me I had scarcely noticed began to wail that his legs ached, his feet were swollen, he couldn't continue another step, he must stop now, give up and lie down. I shouted at him, 'Carry on! Just keep moving! I'll help you.' I seized him by the arm. He was crying, and he told me to let him go, let him be. He pulled himself free of me, falling into the ditch as if he already knew this would be his grave. A rifle cracked.

On the afternoon of this second day we reached the small town of Gleiwitz. My group was put inside a brick factory, where I fell on to a bare patch of ground and huddled close to the prisoner beside me.

Soon came the enraged shouts to get on our feet, but the person sleeping next to me did not move. I shook him, I touched his face and hands, which were icy cold, but he did not move. Then I saw that he bore the red triangle of a political prisoner, inscribed with an 'F', signifying that he was a Frenchman. Almost certainly he had been a communist, but what he had been was of no importance now, to him or to me. But the red triangle that marked his offence, that might save my life: any symbol was better than the yellow star. Quickly I tore the triangle off and searched his pockets looking for any food, but found only a rusty pin. Still, this was a useful find. I pulled off my star, and set the triangle in its place with the pin. Now I am no longer a Jew, I thought. By this stage of the war I probably gained little by this action. The man's blanket almost certainly helped me more.

At last, at the line-up, we were given some hot soup and a piece of bread. The SS men went back into the brick factory and random shots rang out as they made sure of those who had not stirred. We were marched to the railway station and loaded into open cattle wagons. We were squeezed in so tightly we were hardly able to sit. It started to snow again. We each had our blanket – I had my two – and we pulled them over our heads. I do not remember how many days and nights we travelled. We sucked snow to quench our thirst. Many continued to die, and to make more room we piled their bodies at one end where they stank horribly.

At one place, where we were fortunate enough to get some hot soup, I asked an SS man if we could remove the bodies, but the door slammed shut.

As the journey continued westwards I was astonished to see that we were passing through Vienna, for there before my eyes was the famous landmark of the Riesenrad, the Ferris wheel in the Prater fairground, set high against the dusky sky. For the first time since I had left my family behind at the railway station four years ago, I, who had forgotten what tears were, began to cry. Yet how quickly tears were succeeded by anger! And my anger was not aimed at our inhuman persecutors, but at my all too human parents, who had foolishly ignored my plea to leave with me. With them my anger found a manageable target. Though I did not know it, they were already dead, gassed in Auschwitz-Birkenau during my own time there.

We thanked God that we were in open wagons so that some of the stench of excrement and death was carried away on the bitterly cold air. After more days and nights the train stopped and we were given soup and bread.

I lost all sense of time until we arrived at our destination, which was called Mittelbau-Dora and was, I later discovered, near Nordhausen. The wagons were surrounded by SS men. They flung open the doors and backed away as they had at Auschwitz as the odour engulfed them. We could scarcely stand, though the SS soon recovered their shouting voices and used whips and blows to drive us once more from the wagons. We hardly registered any of it.

The rows of five we now stood in once again were far fewer; it seemed to me that more than half of us had died on the journey.

We were led to a building, where we were ordered to strip, and then taken to a long, enclosed room with hundreds of shower heads. We were all familiar with the rumours of the gas chambers disguised as shower rooms, and I was beyond caring whether this chamber would be the place of my end or not, but when the showers hissed, it was water, hot water, which splashed

203

down on us. Evidently the Nazis had further use for us. All too soon we were driven naked from the showers, ordered to put our trousers and jackets back on and taken to another room. Here a doctor, himself a prisoner, examined us.

We were housed in a block once more. This one was at least reasonably well heated, which boosted our morale considerably. We received soup and a piece of bread and I fell asleep on the bunk at once, even though its base was made merely of wooden planks and not even the straw mattress of Buna. I have no memory of my bunk companion.

Next morning, along with ersatz coffee and the piece of bread, we received a slice of salami, an unexpected delicacy. Most of the prisoners I saw looked reasonably well. There were no *Kapos* here, nor a single *Muselmann* either, and though some of our incoming number made up for that soon enough, by this stage of the war the concentration-camp system as we had known it was over. We were now at a place where they produced rockets in underground tunnels.[1] There were SS men everywhere. My job was to push trolleys on rails from one section of the tunnel to the other. There were Russian POWs in faded uniforms working there, with the initials 'KG' (*Kriegsgefangene*, prisoner of war) on the back of their jacket. We and the Russians were slave labourers, but there were volunteer labourers from France, Belgium and other countries there. No doubt my red triangle did assist me in my relations with the Russians, who had little love of Jews.

At first I was pleased to be at Dora, because there was no shouting or beating and the work was easier. Even the Jewish prisoners I saw on my arrival seemed to be in reasonable condition. On our shift we mingled with foreign and volunteer workers. I remember speaking to a number of French volunteers in the tunnel. We ate the same food as the foreign workers, good, thick soup with potatoes and vegetables, superior to the thin liquid we received when off duty. Work was in two long shifts, the first from six in the morning to six at night and the second from six at night until six in the morning. When there were air raids we slept uncomfortably in the tunnel, on the ground without a blanket.

Discipline was brutal and sadistic. One day we were lined up in the tunnel. A French Jew whom I recognised from Buna was brought out. There was a trestle nearby. The Commandant addressed us: 'This man was caught urinating on some machinery in the tunnel. For this he will receive twenty five blows with the truncheon.' The man was made to lower his trousers and bend over the trestle, to which he was bound hand and foot. The SS men chanted malevolently, over and over, '*Fünfundzwanzig am Arsch! Fünfundzwanzig am Arsch!* Twenty-five on the arse!' The Commandant ordered the punishment to begin and the truncheon was passed like a relay baton from SS man to SS man, and I could see the cruel relish in their faces as they struck their helpless victim. His screams of pain turned to whimpers and groans and he was silent for the last few blows. He was taken away on a stretcher to the *Krankenbau* and I did not see him again.

Greater brutality was to come. There was organised sabotage of the rockets by the workers. We heard that they introduced sand into the rocket mechanisms. When a rocket was sabotaged gruesome executions followed, which we were made to watch. Short ropes attached to hooks were placed around the workers' necks. The very electrical mechanism used to lift heavy parts of the rockets was activated and lifted the hooks slowly from the ground. We had to watch as the victims choked to death, struggling and writhing until their final spasmodic jerks. I learnt that it took a man approximately five minutes to die in this manner. Afterwards we had to parade past the bodies. On one occasion a particularly large number of workers, including Russian prisoners, Jews, and civilian workers, were executed. After we had been made to stand and watch, other workers took our place to witness a further batch of executions. By this stage of the war, though, I was hardened to the sight of death, however horribly a person came by it.

As time passed we began to notice the increasing nervousness of our masters, the same signs I had seen at Auschwitz. Once again, with rising hope, we heard the boom of artillery, but conditions at Dora began to worsen as we were fed ever more spasmodically. One day we were given a double ration of bread and the next nothing at all. Soup was no more than a grey liquid, and the margarine and odd piece of sausage we had sometimes received ceased completely. The whole system was collapsing around us. We stood in random groups, speculating once again. One of my group feared the worst. 'Perhaps we will not survive the defeat of the Germans. Perhaps the SS will take us into the tunnel and blow the mountain up over our heads.' As always, I hoped for the best. 'No! Of course we will survive. The Germans aren't going to murder of thousands of prisoners. And if they try that we must fight them with whatever we can lay our hands on, and take as many of them with us as we can.' There were noises of support for me.

And then, one day towards the end of March 1945, when I

had been at Dora for two months, we were once again loaded on to cattle wagons.

A short while into our journey we stopped, the scream of sirens announcing an air raid. Then we journeyed on, hearing the retreating drone of planes overhead. Now, with the temporary distraction of this incident removed, the thirst returned to plague us again. And once more death and excrement began to fill the wagon. At one point in the night the doors rolled back and we received soup and bread. Once in a while we stopped for meagre refreshment at a village, where the local inhabitants seemed unsurprised to see these skeletons in striped pyjamas.

We were five days on that wagon before we finally arrived at Bergen-Belsen. The camp, about 60 kilometres north-east of Hanover, was vast and crammed full. My group was put into a brick barracks formerly used by soldiers. Other prisoners were put in the usual wooden buildings.

Bergen-Belsen was simply a camp of death. There was no work and fewer beatings and, as there was no running water in the latrines because they were blocked and overflowing, the stench of excrement filled the entire camp. The water in the washrooms was polluted. The only drinkable water was from a solitary tap in what was the kitchen area, where you had to stand for several hours to obtain a cup of water. We were now, in truth, less than human. We spent the time picking lice from our bodies. There were *Kapos* at first, and we were provided with some soup, but as the organisation in the camp began to collapse, food became intermittent, appearing one day but not the next.

Soon typhus ran riot. People died in their bunks or wherever they sat, sometimes in their own faeces. I helped to carry out those who had died inside the block, and to pile them up in front of the building. At first we did this neatly, with respect, but as the number of dead rose and we became weaker we just dropped them anywhere outside. Eventually it was too much effort to move them at all.

I contracted typhus and drifted around aimlessly. One day I heard that a cache of turnips had been found buried near the kitchen block. Anyone who could move went to the spot and scrabbled frantically in the earth. I got some and gorged on them, but this only seemed to stimulate my illness and I was racked with pain.

On another occasion I saw two young men doing something strange. They were tracking an inmate who was moving in a slow, staggering motion as if in a drunken stupor. I well knew that this was the prelude to death. When the man collapsed and lay still, the two men fell on him at once, cutting flesh from his body with a knife. They ran away like thieves in the night and, still not understanding, I followed them to where they had vanished behind a block. Here I saw a few flames, over which the two men started to cook the hacked-off meat. Sickened, I turned away, only wanting the agony of life to end.

Overhead, day and night, the sky was darkened with the shapes of Allied bombers. Sometimes German fighters attacked the bombers. We saw crippled planes falling from the skies.

The SS disappeared, and in their place men with different insignia guarded us. All I knew was that they were SS auxiliaries from Central European countries. There were few *Kapos* now, but our captors no longer provided any food.

I, too, became a 'staggerer', and was compelled to sit down ever more frequently. I registered the sound of battle coming ever nearer but it was all as if in a dream. Thirst, starvation and illness were my only realities. The rest concerned me no longer.

On 15 April 1945, two days before my twenty-fourth birthday, and about three weeks since I had entered Belsen, one of the inmates dragged himself into our block, whispering that there was an Allied tank at the gates of the camp. I did not believe him, but went outside anyway and was confronted with an apparition: soldiers surrounding SS men.

The British had liberated us, yet nobody cheered. Eerie silence marked the moment of our liberation. We were too weak, and had experienced too much, to feel joy. It was only when the British distributed a bowl of rice and hot milk that we understood that we might one day be human beings again. The soldiers smiled kindly and we tried to smile back. They warned us to eat slowly, and as little as possible. Sound advice, which some simply could not follow. These were the ones who gorged and died of excess. The British made the SS dig mass graves for the numerous dead scattered around the compound. They forced them to carry the bodies of their victims. It was a heartening sight to see our tormentors forced to work, and under the goad of a rifle barrel if they refused.

I heard that there was a British officer, a rabbi, who was speaking German to inmates. I found the man, Captain Hardman, who told me he came from London. He pointed to my red triangle and asked if I was Jewish. I explained how I had come upon the triangle.

'Where are you from?' he asked.

'I am from Vienna, all my family lived there.'

Reverend Hardman told me that Vienna was now occupied by the Russians, and that Hitler had made the city completely free of Jews, *Judenfrei*.

'I have some relatives who got away to France. Perhaps they're still there,' I said.

'Where would you like to go?'

'I have a brother in America, another got to England. Perhaps one of those countries.' Reverend Hardman wrote everything down.

We remained in the quarantined camp. Our liberators had supplied us with various medicines to restore us, to be taken three times a day. Slowly my health returned, my strength increased and my apathy fell away from me.

One day an officer asked me if I wanted to join a group of inmates who were going on a foraging expedition for food at local farms. There were around fifteen former *Häftlinge* from Bergen-Belsen, all in our conspicuous prisoner's stripes. I leaped at the chance to see the world beyond the camp for the first time in three years. We were on foot, pushing a single trolley and accompanied by a British soldier. We came to a farm close by, where two women and a man, the farmer, met us. Heated discussion quickly followed between them and the soldier. The soldier told us to go into the farmhouse and the outbuildings and take whatever food we could find. I went into the kitchen, where I found sugar, flour and tins of vegetables, which I loaded on to the trolley standing outside. All the time the farmer and the women watched, talking excitedly among themselves. When I returned to the kitchen to continue my search I discovered a large portrait of Hitler hidden behind a storage cupboard. I found a kitchen knife and took the portrait to the soldier, who was outside with the farmer and the women. I slashed the portrait. The farmer spat at me and shouted, '*Du sau Jud!*' A rage such as I have never experienced

210

seized me, and I pushed the knife into his stomach. The soldier intervened at once, shouting at me, and ordering us all out of the place. I do not know how seriously I injured the farmer. One week later I was assigned to the first transport returning to France.

9

VIVE LA VIE

WHAT A strange group of human beings we must have seemed to the outside world, clothed in our camp stripes, but singing! singing! – on the train to Paris, and then on the bus from the train. All the popular songs we knew from before, 'Au près de ma Blonde', J'attendrai' – and how poignant was that title if we had stopped to reflect on it. People in the street waved at us, not seeming to take in our odd appearance. Perhaps it was because we were also singing the *Marseillaise*, or perhaps they were simply catching our mood.

We were billeted in the Hôtel Lutecia on Boulevard Raspail. They offered us food when we arrived, but we refused. Suddenly there was too much food! Ever since liberation everyone had been feeding us. They wanted us to be normal again, like them, but we were not like them. They gave me a room and when I closed the door I realised that I was alone for the first time in years. Here a bed was prepared, with white sheets and a pillow.

From the bathroom came steam – some unknown hand had already run a bath. How strange, how wonderful, that these things had been done for me!

I stood naked, and entered the bath almost reverentially. The warmth of the water was like a drug and I fell asleep, waking with a start when I swallowed water. I washed my body quickly. I dried myself with the towel they had provided, fell into bed and slept a whole day.

The dressing gown hanging behind the door meant that I did not have to put on the stripes when I went downstairs the next morning. There was a good breakfast provided. Officials were interviewing several of our number. When my turn came I was issued with an identification card by the Fédération Nationale des Centres d'Entraide des Internés et Déportés Politiques (National Federation of Mutual Aid Centres for Political Internees and Deportees), which entitled me to free public transport, double food rations and a complete set of clothes, the latter available from a storage area at the hotel. A doctor examined me. I now weighed 49 kilograms. At liberation I had weighed 41 kilograms. The same doctor gave me a voucher for a pair of glasses and told me he would make arrangements for my recuperation in the country. We were given money, ration cards and a laissez-passer as a *'prisonnier politique'*, which gave us free travel on the public transport system.

I collected the suit, went to my room and immediately changed into it, but in the mirror I saw a stranger. The person I knew was the one in camp stripes. It was in those that I looked normal. This suit swamped me. 'You scarecrow,' my reflected image seemed to mock, 'take that suit off! No suit will make you look fat again.

Suits are not meant for you, as you can clearly see!' Later I had my stripes cleaned, as a memento of that life which had once been normal. It was only when I went to America in 1947 that I could bring myself to cut them up, save for a piece of my jacket with my number and the red triangle of the nameless dead French political prisoner, both of which I have to this day.

I did not feel ready to go out into the world on my own and the other *Häftlinge* felt the same. We just sat around in the hotel in our outsize clothing getting to know each other, discussing our possible futures.

It was here that I met Yvonne, another survivor of Auschwitz. We had a short, intense affair, born of that history which bound us together but about which we never spoke. She was older than me, soon to set off in search of her husband and family in the South of France. We promised to keep in touch and soon after she left she sent me three photographs, clearly taken before her deportation. Each had an inscription. One read:

42114 pour 157103 en souvenir d'un passé tragique, mais d'un avenir aux horizons immenses! Vive la vie, avec toute mon amitié plus durable que la paix du monde. Yvonne Avril 1945 (42114 to 157103 in memory of a tragic past, but of a great future! Hurray for life, with all my friendship, longer lasting than the peace of the world)

The date shows that this affair took place a mere few weeks after my liberation from Belsen.

In her last card Yvonne offered me '*toute ma gaîté et mon amour*'. I do not know whether she found her family. I did not reply to her and I cannot now be sure that she even sent me a return address. In the catastrophe which had befallen us our encounter was meant to have been this fleeting thing: we had been just two surviving specks, who had met and touched and loved for a while,

215

and so learnt again that we were human after all, enough for our separate roads ahead, our *'avenir aux horizons immenses'*.

I went to the American embassy to find out if they could help me locate Eric. I was taken under the wing of a very sympathetic vice-consul called Mrs Dix. As I had told Reverend Hardman, I explained that I had no knowledge of the fate of Otto or of my parents, or any of my family save Eric. Otto was young, perhaps he had somehow managed to escape, but all I could tell Mrs Dix was that he had gone to Holland hoping to escape to England. She was fascinated by my story and promised to do her best to find Eric. I have fond memories of this exceptionally kind woman.

Meanwhile the French authorities had found a place for me to recuperate, with a family in a village. I informed the American embassy of my new address and boarded a train to the village of Salornay-sur-Guye, in the eastern *département* of Saône-et-Loire.

My sponsor was a Dr Bennetin. He and his family received me warmly. In fact the entire village seemed to come out to meet me. They asked me about my time in the camps. I did not want to talk about this and they did not persist, and so the pattern of my silence was set. At night I slept in a large room on a double bed in the Bennetins' beautiful home.

Dr Bennetin understood my silence but, obviously wanting some token of my war, he asked me if he might photograph me in my camp uniform. Looking back from the perspective of today, these photographs of a reasonably healthy-looking individual dressed up in those terrible pyjamas may seem to be in poor taste, but at the time I believe there was no prurience in the good doctor's request. It is for this reason that I reproduce the photographs here.

I met Janine, the chemist's daughter, and her family. I was attracted to Janine, but I only got so far with her, try as I might.

This pursuit of pleasure may seem strange to the reader. I had until recently lived for two years in the depths of human depravity and had emerged a skeleton. Nor did I know what had befallen nearly all my family; yet I seemed to seek only pleasure. How can I explain it? At one level, I am sure, I was driven to seize life with all the returning strength of my young manhood, all but stolen by the Nazis. At another, deeper level I was attempting to obliterate, or at least distract myself from, the past and the terrible possibilities of the present. I did not want to think beyond the moment. I fell easily into that way of being. After all, this is how one had learnt to live in the *Lager*, without history, without thought, and with no wider hope than to live one more day.

One day, some weeks after my arrival in Salornay, I was strolling with Janine when we saw a man in uniform talking to a group of villagers. Curious, we approached, and to my astonishment I recognised my brother Eric. I cried out his name and in an instant we were in each other's arms. It was almost impossible to take in that I was once again embracing my own flesh and blood. We walked to the Bennetins', so overwhelmed with the joy of this reunion, with so much to ask one another, and such a sense of an age of different experiences separating us since we had bade farewell in Vienna, that we were almost silent. 'Is Otto still in England?' I asked at one point. 'No, he came to America just before the war started. He lives in Brooklyn now.'

Eric told me how he had found me. His commanding officer had permitted him to visit all the camps where it was possible I had been. At Bergen-Belsen he discovered that I was alive and he had followed my route to Paris. There my fairy godmother, Mrs Dix at the American embassy, told him where I was. 'What a walk

I've had this morning getting here after I got off the train at ... what's the name of the place?' Eric asked.

'It must have been Mâcon, or Tournus?' I said

'I don't know. Anyway, it was far.'

We spoke of our parents. 'The last letter I got from them was at the start of 1941,' said Eric. 'I can't go to Vienna because the Russians are there. I've been told there are no Jews there now.'

I was the one who knew what it was like in the camps. My father would have been nearly sixty, and my mother in her mid-fifties. There were no old people in Auschwitz when I was there, except for distinguished persons like Professor Waitz. But I was as reluctant to speak about my war to my own brother as I was to the strangers around me. The past was dead, locked away. I knew that Eric must have seen the condition of the people in the camps when he was searching for me, but I told myself that I was no longer one of those people. 'It was tough, very bad,' was all I wanted to say about it.

Eric spent two days with me at the Bennetins', sharing my room. They welcomed him with open arms, though conversation between them was mainly by way of nods and smiles, with some translation by me.

'I'm married now,' Eric told me. 'Her name is Vivian. You want to know something? Vivian is a distant relative of ours.'

'How?'

'Her maiden name is Dreiband. One of our grandfather's sisters married a Dreiband. Their son lived in Pszemisl, in Poland, and emigrated to America at the beginning of the century.'

In this small way Eric was telling me how, with his new wife, he was going to do his small part to carry on that long history of the Jews, that he would have children with her, that the Nazis and

218

those like them would never realise their dream of a world without Jews, because the human spirit was stronger than their hatred, because although we had lost our parents, yet others of their generation had survived, just as we, their descendants, had.

I was seized by my old restlessness and decided it was time to leave this peaceful village. Eric himself had to rejoin his unit in Germany after a short two days' leave. 'Otto and I are going to get you over to the States,' he promised.

He promised that he and Otto were going to do everything he could to obtain a visa for me for America. I promised the kindly Bennetins that I would keep in touch and left the shelter of their hospitality. I had been with them for just one month. I took the train south in search of the Bodeks, but felt compelled to visit Figeac in search of Jacqueline, who I was convinced had betrayed me, and to discover the truth about my arrest. I went to the bistro where she and I had often met and recognised the owner. Yes, he told me, he knew Jacqueline, she had often come in with a German officer. Maybe she had gone with him when the Germans retreated, so many of the women who had gone with Germans – they didn't want to hang around did they, the traitors?

There was nothing to keep me in Figeac, so I took the train to Nice. At the Jewish Community Centre there, where my *laissez-passer* entitled me to a little money and a meal, I was eating with other refugees when I heard the familiar voice of my cousin Leo from an adjoining table. More astonishment, more joy, and with him was his new wife, Annie. Leo told me that his parents (my Uncle Hermann and Aunt Genya) had been deported by the Vichy government, but that Rosi, who had got her husband, Max, out of St Cyprien, was living safely with him and Maxl in Limoges. We now knew of the gassings, but it was a long time before we knew for certain that all our parents had perished. We were luckier than many, for at least some of our family had been spared.

We left for Limoges the same day. Leo told me his story during the journey:

'Maxl and I tried to escape to Switzerland from France in 1943. We had false papers, describing us as of French nationality but born in Switzerland – and, of course, we really had been born there. We changed our name a little – just enough, I think, from Bodck to Bodec. Well, the Swiss caught us just over the border and put us in the hands of the German border guards. The German authorities suggested we work in Germany – we would be well paid there. We told them we would think about it, and we left for Lyons, because we wanted to meet cousin Jonas Tempelhof, who had paid for our false papers. By pure chance we ran into him at the station – he was returning to his family in Neuchâtel. Well, there wasn't much he could do for us and so we stayed in Nice. I got a job there with a Jewish furrier, and Maxl with a Jewish tailor. It was all a mess, and really very ironic. Our employers actually knew we were Jewish, but what they were afraid of was getting into trouble with the authorities for hiring "French" staff, which was illegal for Jewish businesses.

'Anyway, I met Annie in Lyon. She was born in Paris, but her family, who were Polish, were deported from Drancy. Annie was living with a Christian family, who were worried that it would be discovered they were hiding a Jewess. So Annie, alone, left for Lyons. We fell in love and started living together. Vichy started making life impossible for Jews, so we decided we would volunteer to work in Germany. Incredible as it seems, we all thought it was a better option.

'So in February 1943, we were shipped to "Ostmark" – Austria, "our country", and we worked as labourers in a factory near Semmering, the Goering Werke. Annie worked as a domestic in the houses of German workers. When the Germans discovered we spoke perfect German, we got a much better job, as interpreters for the French volunteers there, and there were a lot of them. Our real problem was Annie. She would insist that she spoke perfect German. If it weren't so dangerous, it would have been comic, her stubbornness over this. We knew that what she was speaking was really the Germanised Yiddish of her parents. The director there was a Herr Witzmann, and we got on very well with him.

'One day – I seem to remember it was in July, or around there, but definitely 1943 – he invited Maxl and me for coffee at his home. There was some talk about the attempt on Hitler's life – which is why I date it around then – when Herr Witzmann remarked that it was a pity the attempt had not succeeded. Maxl and I were completely flabbergasted. Witzmann said, "Look, I know you are Jewish, my own brother-in-law is Jewish. You have nothing to fear from me. You'll be safe here." Annie got pregnant, but Klara, our daughter died. Afterwards, we were repatriated to France and married. We were in Nice to find out about Annie's parents…'

By the time we reached Limoges, a long journey, and I had fallen into the arms of Rosi, Max and my cousin Maxl and told them of my reunion with Eric, I was exhausted with emotion. Yet how little changed they all seemed to me, and I began to wonder how I seemed to them. They did not press me for details of my experiences. I mentioned the camps, but said not much more. I could only marvel at how we, the younger generation, had come through the evil of these times.

My cousins advised me to register with Le Comité Juif d'Assistance Sociale et de Reconstruction, where I would receive a ration card and an allowance as a deported survivor. Another survivor, Leo Bretholz, interviewed me. He was also from Vienna. 'Yes, I was in Drancy, too, but I jumped from the train on the way to Auschwitz.' He said no more, and I remembered how we had started making a hole in our wagon but had given up the idea. We became friends. Leo had family in America and, like me, was waiting for papers to emigrate. Later he was to write an account of his survival. We spent a lot of time together. At parties we sang together – his voice was wonderful – and pursued girls.

In May 1946 I was offered a job as an interpreter with the US Army. The 3046 Grave Registration company had the task of searching for unmarked graves of Allied personnel. German POWs were used to exhume the bodies for transport to their country of origin. The evidence of German atrocities was common knowledge by now, and they were hated. A black sergeant in the company told me I had the chance to repay the Germans for what they had done to me. He laughed when he pointedly told me I would always have an armed escort behind me.

Two guards accompanied the eight prisoners in our detail on that first day. 'Make the bastards work hard,' said these guards, and I knew that they were giving me direct authority over the prisoners. I felt elated. Seven of the prisoners seemed meek, but the eighth caught my eye. All the prisoners must have known I was a Jew, but this one displayed his contempt for me in every gesture and glance. He moved and worked slowly at my command. I shouted, *'Arbeit schneller, Ihr Schweine Hunde!'*, just as I had been yelled at in the camps. They all worked faster, except him. He muttered something. I thought I heard '*Sau Jud*'. I marched over to him and asked him what he said. He only smirked and I exploded, punching him in the face. 'You are lucky it is the American army guarding you or you would have been killed by a Jew,' I told him. One of the guards clapped me on the shoulder. He was pleased by what I had done.

Leo and I went to the American embassy in Paris for an interview. There the Consul asked us about our life during the war. And, yes, we had to sign papers to say we had never been a member of a fascist organisation – or a communist one. I knew that, with Eric's efforts, my papers would arrive at some point.

So I was in Paris again. Leo and I craved only excitement. I cannot even remember where we stayed. And just as I did not want to think about my parents, so I made no excursion to the Jewish district in search of the Hubermans.

I remember one evening when Leo and I went to the Opéra Comique to see Rossini's *The Barber of Seville*. Afterwards we were drawn to the lights of a fairground in Place de la République and rode dodgem cars. It was here that Leo lost his wallet, which we did not notice until we got home. It contained cash and, more importantly, his Polish passport stamped with a visa for America.[1] We passed a night of terrible anxiety. The next day, more in hope than expectation, we made our way back to the fairground. To our amazement the man who ran the dodgems produced the wallet, its contents intact. He had found it, he told us, while clearing away the previous night. This small, decent action made us feel as if this stranger had restored to us not just the wallet but ourselves, once again, to the human fold. It made us quiet for a while.

It was in Le Havre, in the winter of 1946, that I met my brother

Otto for the first time since our farewell in Vienna. He had become a doctor, just as he had always wanted, but needed a further degree to practise in New York. He was on his way to Switzerland to study for it. 'OK,' he joked, 'you look older at last, so I won't call you my kid brother any more.'

Before he started his studies Otto was going to Zermatt to ski. Would I join him? I hadn't skied since I was a youngster – not that I was especially good at it then – but I was delighted to join my brother.

Eric and I had been together for only two days in Salornay, but now that I had two weeks alone with Otto it was hard not to talk in greater detail about my experiences. Besides, Otto had a way of asking very pertinent questions. I told him a lot, but not everything. I refrained from mentioning many of the most traumatic events, which now appear in this book.

In a strange repetition of our youth, it was Otto who found a girlfriend in Zermatt. I flirted with her, and Otto joked and said, 'Hey! You can't do that!' But there was only friendliness in it. Otto later broke with the girl after she made an antisemitic remark.

10

MEETING THE PAST

LEO AND I booked our tickets for America and on Sunday 19 January 1947 we boarded the passenger ship *John Ericson* at Le Havre. I left the shores of Europe for the first time in my life, and with no regret.

The North Atlantic crossing was often very rough and, feeling seasick in our cabin, Leo and I frequently mounted the dangerously wet, swaying steps to march around the deck, and this helped control our nausea. As we ploughed westwards it became bitterly cold and spears of icicles hung from the railings and lifeboats. But below decks there was young company to be enjoyed, including the pleasure of casual flirtation with young French, Belgian and Dutch girls – war brides following their American soldier husbands to the States. There were German war brides, too, but Leo and I – who spoke to each other in French rather than our mother tongue – avoided them. Leo, as flirtatious as me, became especially fond of a French girl called Claudine,

225

who was going to meet her American soldier fiancé. At night we danced to a jazz band.

On Wednesday 29 January everyone crowded on deck as the famous Manhattan skyline grew ever more distinct. Seagulls shrieked overhead. As we passed the Statue of Liberty everyone on the ship shouted and applauded.

My brothers were waiting for me on the dock with their new wives, as was Leo's uncle, Sam Goldstein, with whom he was going to live in Baltimore.

I stayed with Otto, now qualified as a doctor, in a basement flat in President Street, Brooklyn. He had completed his medical studies in Switzerland and had gained his certificate to practise in New York. He had married Lotte, who had escaped from Czechoslovakia to Sweden with her family in 1938.

Eric was also living in Brooklyn at this time, working as a pattern cutter in the fashion industry. We all spent a lot of time together in those first few months and I saw that Eric, always the quietest and least confident of the three of us, had found in his wife Vivian a woman whose devotion and strong personality compensated for his lack of self-esteem. I remember how Eric would often demand of my mother, 'Do you love me? But do you love me?' Vivian and Eric had a son, David, named after our father.

One evening Otto told me that there existed a package from our parents, that Eric had it in his possession and that now was the time to discuss it. So, shortly afterwards at his apartment, Eric produced a large wooden box. Inside was another box and when he opened it I was stunned to see my parents' silver cutlery and various items of Mother's jewellery. I became tearful when I saw the diamond and ruby ring she had always worn, because I had not expected my youth and her past to confront me in so personal and tangible a form. 'It will be yours when you marry,' said my brothers.

It never occurred to me to ask Eric how my parents' valuables had arrived in America. Once I received the letters after Eric's death, the answer was there, in my father's letter to Eric of 18 April 1939 – the day after my birthday, during the time I was in Antwerp. He writes:

'Regarding the piano I am not sure that I am able to send it. I have had a great deal of expense with Otto and am a little short of money at present. All non-Aryans [*Nicht Arier*] have had to give up all gold and silver items. We had to give up our silver candlesticks and some gold items. It is forbidden to export items of rare metals from here. Uncle Menashes from Cairo, who is travelling to Switzerland to take a cure, will send you a packet of black chocolate. Enjoy it.'

The mention of 'black chocolate' is almost certainly a reference to the Yiddish phrase *schwarze geld*, illegal money. So it was Uncle Menashes, who had sent me £2 per month from Cairo when I was in Antwerp, who had also sent my parent's valuables on to America. How this was accomplished will never be known. Perhaps he visited my parents in Vienna, received the items from them and then forwarded them from Switzerland, where he was indeed taking a cure.

I started to take evening classes in English and became a filing clerk in a Manhattan finance company. I kept in touch with Leo Bretholz, who had settled in Baltimore.

It was about a year after I arrived in America that Leo called to tell me that there was a vacancy in the textile firm where he worked as a salesman. I left New York and joined the Standard Textile Company of Baltimore. I moved into Leo's little

227

apartment. Living with us was another Viennese immigrant, Fred Jacob. Traditional Friday-night dinners were resumed with Leo's Uncle Ossi and Aunt Olga. Yet another Viennese refugee in our circle was Herbert Friedman.

So it was that in Baltimore, as in Vienna, I was once again living almost exclusively among Jews. To this day it remains a fact that almost all my friends are Jews. The atmosphere of my childhood and later experiences have made it so.

One morning a girl in our circle contacted me. 'Would you like to meet a girl from the Old Country?' she asked. The 'Old Country' was the expression American Jews used to describe the whole of Europe. The girl was Freda, who was from England. I called her on Monday 9 October 1950, was fascinated by her English accent, and fell in love there and then, on the telephone.

Leo shook his head. Even by my standards of impulsiveness this was extreme. 'You don't think things through,' he said, 'and anyway you are crazy – you don't even know what the girl looks like.'

Freda and I met that same month and within four weeks I proposed to her. I told her I wanted her to have my mother's ring. Her father flew out at once to New York waving a ticket for her flight home. Who was I? he said; only a refugee with few prospects.

Freda stood firm, and so her father stayed in New York for a while, perhaps hoping to change her mind. In the end we must have convinced him that this was not a flash in the pan, because he paid for our engagement party at Zimmerman's Hungaria Restaurant on West 46th Street, where they played gypsy music and my future father-in-law got to know my brothers, whom he found it hard to dislike.

On leaving, in a last-ditch attempt to get his beloved daughter to come home, he said, 'Why don't you both come to England?

And Freda, you will miss your family, you will not be happy here.' Freda and I married on 31 December, only two months after meeting. There was a reason, apart from love, for this speed. There was a $400-dollar tax rebate for newly-weds, a lot of money for us in those days. Marrying on the last day of the year meant that we could get the maximum tax relief.

On 9th June 1952 I became an American citizen. It was yet another place, another adventure. The Nazis had achieved something in my case, turning me into the Wandering Jew of antisemitic mythology. But having no homeland had its compensations: I could settle anywhere.

Freda's father, Mark, was right in his prediction. I was doing well at Standard Textiles and Freda in her radio work, but it was painfully clear that she missed her family greatly. So, on 1 July that same year, we left for England on the *Queen Elizabeth*.

At first we lived with Freda's family in Hendon, north London. But, when we were hunting for our own home, our estate agent noticed my accent and, after asking me where I was from, said, 'I know a Viennese, do you think you might know him?' This turned out to be Freddie Breitfeld, now Bradfield, that friend of my youth whose parents had been wise enough to move their business to England before it was too late. Freddie I and met again and he and his wife, Susi, became very close friends of ours.

Two years after I had settled in England, Freda and I were strolling through the West End one afternoon. We stopped outside a restaurant in Duke Street called Ici Paris, thinking perhaps to eat there. I glanced at the display case and saw a photograph of a woman singing. My heart raced as I realised that

I was looking at Minna Huberman. Thirteen years on, she seemed hardly changed. The restaurant was closed that day, so we took the telephone number, booked the following day and returned that very evening.

It was Minna who greeted us. I began to speak to her in French. I told her my name, I mentioned Chez Huberman, her parents, Otto Geringer. Minna gazed at me. 'Is it really you, Freddie?' We embraced, almost in disbelief. She took us to our table and then joined us, introducing her husband, a Corsican gentile, who, we later discovered, had saved her from deportation. The remainder of Minna's story was a familiar one: her parents had been deported in 1942, and she had never seen them again. The four of us shared a meal and the occasion was treated as a joyous reunion, but Minna and I made no arrangement to meet again, because what connected us but the very events we wanted to forget? Minna sang later that evening, some of the old Edith Piaf songs she used to sing in Paris in 1941, after the last customer had left Chez Huberman and Otto would look on adoringly, dreaming his hopeless dream of seducing her.

It was twenty years later, in 1974, when I was just starting to speak about my former life, that I felt the urge to meet Minna again. I made my way to the restaurant, but it no longer existed. I had lost her.

By then I had learnt that silence about one's past does not bring forgetfulness and that its pressure becomes like the pressure of fire in the belly of a volcano.

In 1979 I travelled to Paris to see my cousins Maxl and Rosi, but there was another person I wanted very much to visit. I had traced Professor Robert Waitz through Amicale d'Auschwitz et des Camps de Haute-Silésie, and the address they gave me was in the heart of Paris. An elegant woman opened the door and I explained who I was. She smiled and asked me in. She told me that her husband had died only a few months previously. He had been ill at liberation, but had made a good recovery. I was so sorry, I told her, and wanted her to know that I owed my life to her husband, that I would never forget his kindness. She cried, and said, yes, he had been a wonderful man. She told me that she herself had survived the war by hiding in the Unoccupied Zone, but I cannot remember the details of her story. We drank coffee and talked for a long time. I had so wanted to see Professor Waitz, and I felt overwhelmingly sad when I finally bade farewell to his wife and walked through the city of Paris, which, but for him, I would surely never have seen again.

In the camps I had dreamt of that future time when, free again, I would stand on a platform at some press conference, surrounded by hundreds of journalists, and tell my story to the world. I could not have anticipated the silence of my post-Holocaust self, although the period of this was not so much longer than that of the world at large.

It was only about twenty years after the war that society at last began to consider the scale of the Jewish tragedy. To give the number six million some personal scale, to remove it from the realm of a flat statistic, I make myself think of how many died among my own immediate family and friends. But then it becomes dizzying and hard to grasp again because those friends had families and friends, and so my head spins again as I try to contemplate the web of human relationships destroyed in those years of madness.

Still, I try to count the losses.

231

My own parents were deported from Vienna to Theresienstadt on 2 October 1942 on transport No. 4/12-363, before I left Paris. Where they were between their penultimate letter of 8 January 1941 and their last, undated one will remain unknown. They may never have received the one letter I did send them from Paris, and may never have known I was even there. From Theresienstadt my father and mother were deported to Auschwitz with fifteen hundred other Jews on 19 October 1944. My parents' numbers were respectively ES-559 and ES-560. There were only two further transports from Theresienstadt after that, on 23 and 28 October 1944, which carried a total of 3753 Jews. Although this suggests that my parents came very close to surviving, I have no knowledge of their state of health by then, as conditions in the camp were very poor. The Russians liberated Auschwitz on 27 January 1945.

Neither could I have known that, while I was in the middle of my Paris adventure, the second deportation of Jews from the Vichy camp of Gurs to the Drancy camp in Paris and then on to Auschwitz on 12 August 1942, contained my Uncle Hermann and Aunt Genya. They were just two among the one thousand on that transport.

In 1947 Otto, who was studying in Switzerland, went to Vienna with his wife, Lotte. His purpose was to visit our old apartment there. He found an old couple living there with all our family furniture around them, including Otto's grand piano. They had been assigned the apartment only a year ago, they explained. Otto went to the Kultusgemeinde, where my father had worked after his company had been Aryanised. There he learnt of our parents' deportation. He went to the company which had published his 1937 composition 'Cher Ami, Cher Ami, Ich erwarte Sie' and asked them for a copy of his music. They looked up their record and came back to Otto, telling him that his composition had been burnt, together with those of Felix Mendelssohn. Otto had laughed, 'Just think, me and Mendelssohn, together!'

Miss Schiff, who, after the Anschluss, had been forced to give up her apartment to an Aryan family and move in with my parents, was deported with them to Theresienstadt and subsequently perished in Auschwitz. Our neighbours the Aments, who had telephoned us on Kristallnacht to tell us that our synagogue was in flames, perished, though their children survived and emigrated, like my brother Eric, to America.

Perhaps it is a measure of the shame I have harboured for years about my companion at Chez Huberman, Otto Geringer, that I only recently established through Serge Klarsfeld's book that he had been deported from Drancy on Convoy 50 on 4 March 1943. No asterisk – denoting survival – appears by his name, so it is almost certain that he perished at Auschwitz. His date of birth is given as 14 February 1924. He had been seventeen when I met him, a year younger than me.

Annie, my cousin Leo's wife, learnt that her parents had been deported from Paris and had also perished at Auschwitz.

So many losses. And another is certain aspects of my own memory. My cousin Maxl has reminded me that he was at Eksaarde with me. Just as I wrongly placed him by my side when I left Vienna, so have I reversed matters at Eksaarde. He was there for those three months. He came to be there because in November 1939 the Belgian government decreed that each Jewish refugee family had to send one member to Eksaarde or Merksplas. The Belgian authorities decided Maxl had to go to Eksaarde, probably because he was only eighteen. Maxl now tells me that we played a lot of chess together, and he worked at his tailoring.

Maxl has told me that he and Leo visited me in Paris during the war, but I have no memory of this at all. Obviously I must have been in correspondence with them for them to know where to find me.

The penultimate letter my parents sent, which was to Eric, states:

'Many months have passed and still no letters from you... We want to tell you that, thank God, we are in good health. Regarding Freddy, we have told you before that he went back to Brussels. We have already received two letters from him. He writes that he is, thank God, well. He was even able to get most of his things back but unfortunately his cello is lost... He also briefly visited Antwerp, where he visited Hansi Spitzer, who is married to Torczyner. She wrote to us that Freddy has become very grown up... May God protect him.'

I recall it all, except that I cannot remember my visit to Hansi Spitzer. It seems so strange that Hansi wrote to my parents, and my parents to Eric, and a letter reporting my visit returns like a homing pigeon to me, who has no recollection of the events described.

Nor, more remarkably, do I remember Uncle Hermann and Leo being with me at St Cyprien, but in a letter dated 5 August 1940 they wrote to Eric:

'Dear Erich

...From Fredl, we have received two cards from St Cyprien and today even a letter. He tells us that he is in good health and that he is not short of anything. He writes that he gets plenty of food. Also Uncle and Leo are there, but aunt Genya lives near Toulouse.

Fredy asked one should write to him Post Restante Toulouse. I am asking you, dear Erich, write to Fredy that we are well and that we are temporarily unable to write to him. Tell him also that Maxl remained in Brussels and that he is well... Regarding the registration documents for Fredy, one does not know if he will remain where he is at present. See to it, dear Erich, that the little Fredl will soon be with you...'

Max Schächter, Rosi's husband, and his brother Avraham were also in the camp, both of whom I had visited in Belgium before the invasion.

Pierre Heimrath and I, who became separated on the death march from Auschwitz, fell into each other's arms soon after the war, when we ran into each other at a refugee centre. However, as much as I rack my brains, I cannot recall where this was – only that it was in France, and probably in Nice. We spent some time together, and I know that we avoided all talk of the war. I have been trying, without success, to trace Pierre through the French Holocaust survivors' newspaper. All I have of him is a photograph taken at our reunion.

I visited Paris recently to retrace my course through those streets some sixty years before. As I walked down Rue de Provence I saw a large supermarket stretching along the side of the road where Madame Jamet's famous establishment had been, so I expected number 122 to have been swallowed up. But no, there it was, the number displayed above the large double wooden door, though I cannot say if it is that same door of my youth, as similar as it looks. I stood and gazed at it for a while before turning back down Rue de Provence and stopping on the corner of Rue du Faubourg Montmartre, before crossing into Rue Richer, to browse in a beautiful old confectionery and wine shop, which certainly must have existed during my time here, though I do not remember it. I lingered for some time, but when I crossed the road I discovered that Rue Richer still remains a sort of Jewish quarter, though much diluted, with a few Jewish shops, all closed as it was a Saturday.

Beside the Folies Bergère, there was a wide metal gate. Perhaps, behind this gate, was the very courtyard in which Chez Huberman had stood, but there was no way of knowing. The metal gate guarded its secret entirely, and after standing there for a while I turned back along Rue Richer.

I took the Métro to Pigalle and made my way to Rue de Douai, in search of the Hôtel du Collège Rollin, where I had rented my room over sixty years before. The street was exactly as I remembered it, and I was certain that my hotel had been on the right-hand side of the street, about halfway down. The tall windows with their shutters were all familiar to me, but the entrances beneath these windows had different names. I spoke to the owner of one of the hotels. He listened with kindly interest as I told him I had been a refugee here in the war, but of my hotel he knew nothing.

The next day I visited my eighty-seven-year-old cousin, Rosi, now a widow, who was living in a tiny, neat studio flat in a suburb of Paris. She worried about some cakes she had bought for our tea, because she had dropped the box on the pavement.

Rosi, another survivor. Of her escape to Switzerland I had only a vague picture from a letter she had written to her grandchildren, who have chosen an ultra-Orthodox way of life and live in Strasbourg. She wanted them to understand a little of what she and her family had been through.

Her daughter Ruth, who lives next door to her, has isolated

herself entirely from the events surrounding her own birth in Switzerland. The Holocaust is not her story, it is her mother's. She wants none of it. And Rosi's grandchildren, in their Orthodox enclave, have followed their mother's feeling in their own way. We talked over tea and Rosi told me her story, which is a confused one, and there are parts which I have been unable to fit into a coherent chronology. She told her story in a lively way. 'I remember seeing you on the haystack with a pitchfork, helping the farmer,' she said to me fondly at one point, referring to my time with her family near Gaillac. Only once was she overcome, and this was when I showed her a postcard my father had written to Eric from Vienna. At the sight of her uncle's handwriting the scar of the past must have again become a wound and she cried.

One of the nightmares I used to suffer disturbed me more than any. My parents stood by the gas chamber building, placidly queuing to go inside. I screamed at them, 'Don't go in! Please don't go in!' My father just laughed at me and told me not to worry. 'Everything will be all right,' he said.

Yes, that was his nature, blindly optimistic. And mine, too. Perhaps it was a blessing for me, because I always believed that I would survive the camps, and that belief, and a lot of luck, probably did save me. But I had an advantage over my father in that I came to know my enemy unmasked, daily faced the depths of depravity of which he was capable, gauged the amount of effort and ingenuity and sheer deceit required to keep him at bay. And I was young. My father could not conceive of a world gone so utterly mad and, at their age, my parents would not have been given the chance to adapt to Auschwitz. They would have been useless and immediately expendable specimens to the Nazis.

Through the internet a distant Knoller relative contacted me

237

with a story of my parents' last recorded days. In the confusion of those times it is hard to know whether it is fully accurate, partly accurate or simply untrue. When I contacted this relative, Karen Pratt (née Knoller), she said she could not remember who she heard the story from, but it must have been someone in the family. The story has it that my parents had obtained exit visas from Vienna, but some other people, through bribery, succeeded in getting officials to change the names. Later a chance came for my parents to go to Palestine, but this was apparently through some illegal means and so my father would not seize this opportunity. Even if the story is myth, it accurately characterises my father's nature. And so my parents perished, for no other reason than that they were Jews. I have some family photographs, the small pieces of my mother's jewellery I gave to Freda, and the family cutlery, which Lotte gave to me when I married. Apart from these items, I have only memories.

I try to find some grain of meaning in all this, some small hope that human nature can rise above the worst of such horrors. And I do find some such hope in one of my mother's postscripts, in a letter from Eric to Otto dated 6 February 1939, when I was already in Belgium. She adds:

'I must tell you that I have never seen such beautiful photographs as you have sent. Miami looks like a paradise. If possible please send Mr Hagmann a postcard from Miami. Fredy has also sent him a card, and he was very happy to have received it.'

I have long forgotten this small action of mine, and neither do my mother's words stir any memory, but her words surely confirm that I was right to have liked Mr Hagmann.

Remembering Mr Hagmann reminds me of the enthusiasm for stamps I shared with our caretaker and, remembering those happy afternoons, brings me back to a time when I was visiting Eric and Vivian in Florida. 'Do you remember those political stickers I used to collect? The ones father tore up that time?' I did. Eric shook his head sadly. 'What a thing father did.' He smiled. 'They might have been worth a fortune now,' he said.

England, the country where my two daughters were born, Marcia in 1953 and Susie in 1956, has proved to be a kind host, and I am indebted to her. Yet, as if in some echo of the past, both my daughters live abroad, Susie in Israel with our only grandchild, Nadav, and Marcia has recently moved to the Canary Islands, both as restless by choice as I by force of circumstance. So, even now, my family is not around me.

I returned to my cello in this country, playing with a local orchestra for many years. For some years Freda, Marcia and I ran a fashion business. Later, and until my retirement, I was a director with State of Israel Bonds. I continue to work with survivors of the Holocaust in the Holocaust Survivors Centre in London, and speak in schools all over the world about my experiences. It is a mission for me. I will never entirely exorcise the demons of my past, nor do I wish to. I wish only to confront them and in this, I think, I have succeeded.

At the start of this book I dedicated my story to my parents. At the end of it, I should like to add a further dedication to the six million who, unlike me, cannot tell their story.

On 6 June 2000 Freddie Knoller, the Jewish boy who left Vienna in 1938, and became a survivor of Auschwitz and Belsen, took his place at the opening of the permanent Holocaust Exhibition at London's Imperial War Museum and shook hands with the Queen of England.

APPENDIX 1

ROSI'S STORY

WE LEFT Vienna in 1938, first my brothers, Leo and Maxl in August, and then my parents and me. My fiancé, Max, had been arrested [he was of Polish origin]. I sent him a registered letter, asking him to send his passport as I was making arrangements to get him a visa to Santo Domingo [in the Dominican Republic]. He presented this letter to the prison authorities, who gave him twenty-four hours to leave the country. In this way we were reunited in Belgium. He came with his mother. After the German invasion of Belgium we all escaped to France, where we were separated and interned as enemy aliens. The men were sent to St Cyprien and the women to a camp near Gaillac. I cannot remember its name. Without permission or papers [a *sauve-conduit*] I left the camp and went to St Cyprien to get my husband out if I possibly could. Fredy was there also. I became ill with heatstroke and was put in hospital at the camp. They wanted me to leave the camp when I had recovered, but I

241

refused to do so without my husband. I was able to produce some proof that I could support him financially as I had a small inheritance from my grandfather Kernberg in Switzerland. My brother Leo and my father were also able to leave, as Leo had been born in Switzerland.

During the time we stayed near Gaillac, I remember Fredy on the top of a hay wagon, working for the farmer, a pitchfork in his hands. After Leo left, Fredy followed, and it was now that the mayor started to make life very difficult for the Jews. He decided to put all of us in a camp near Gaillac. Max and I bribed a guard to let us and Max's mother out. This bribe was supposed to include my parents, but there was a change of guard, and they could not leave. I now know that they were taken with other Jews to Gurs, and from there to Drancy and Auschwitz.

…When we left Gaillac we made our way to Nice. We had no papers, and there were many round-ups of foreign Jews. I had married Max in Belgium and now I was pregnant with my daughter Ruth. Naturally, we were terrified of deportation. I got a certificate from a doctor that I was pregnant and managed to get some papers declaring that I was a Polish citizen. As I had some documentation now, I persuaded Max that we should try to cross the border to Switzerland. He was not so keen. In the end, he agreed. We got to Aix-en-Provence. By this time Maxl and Leo had tried and failed to get into Switzerland. They were in jail in Aix-en-Provence. I asked a Jewish-looking man if he knew the camp for Jews being deported East. He told me the Jews went yesterday. I asked if he knew the Bodek brothers and he said, 'Ah, the Swiss, no, they were not deported.' There were no buses, and we managed to get a ride in a car to the camp, which was some way outside the town. I found my brothers. We had found another Swiss relative in France, Johnny [Jonas] Tempelhof, and he arranged for Maxl and Leo to be called to the Swiss embassy. Gendarmes accompanied them to the embassy, which was in Marseilles. Johnny bribed the gendarmes to allow them to go for a cup of coffee with him. They took their chance and ran away. It was Johnny who arranged their false papers, which enabled them to work as volunteers in Germany. Johnny had told me and Max about a guide in Annemasse. We went there, but decided to cross the border on our own. We had extraordinary luck. There was a milkman. He said, 'You go this way,' and there we were, safe in Switzerland. The Swiss police stole all our valuables. Max was sent to work in a refugee camp and I was cared for with great kindness by a religious Christian Swiss family. I have to say that my own relatives in Switzerland did not choose to help us. There, in Switzerland, Ruth was born.

APPENDIX 2

CHRONOLOGY

1921
17 *April – Freddie Knoller is born.*

1933
March – President Hindenburg appoints Adolf Hitler
Reichs Chancellor of Germany.

1934
25 July – An attempted coup in Vienna by the
Nazi Party is foiled, but the Austrian Chancellor, Engelbert
Dollfuss, is assassinated.

1935
The German Reichstag passes the antisemitic Nuremberg
Laws.

1936
17 July – Spanish fascists stage a military coup against
the Republican.

government in Madrid, leading to the Spanish civil war.
25 November – Germany and Japan sign the Anti-Comintern Pact, opposing the Communist International.

1937

6 November – Italy joins the Anti-Comintern Pact.

1938

11 March – The Anschluss – Germany takes over Austria, which becomes Ostmark.
9 November – Kristallnacht, or 'Night of Broken Glass'.
23 *November – Freddie leaves his parents in Vienna and goes to Belgium.*
7 *December – Eric Knoller sails to the USA.*

1939

April – Otto Knoller leaves Austria for England via Holland.
August – Freddie is taken to the Merksplas refugee camp in Belgium.
1 September – German troops invade Poland.
3 September – Britain and France declare war on Germany.

1940

February – Freddie is taken to the Eksaarde refugee camp in Belgium.
February – Otto sails from England to the USA.
10 May – Belgium is invaded by German troops. *Freddie flees to France.*
12 *May – Freddie is arrested by the French as an enemy alien and taken to the St Cyprien internment camp, near Perpignan.*
13 May – Germany invades France.

14 June – German troops enter Paris.

22 June – The German–French armistice is signed at
Compiègne, near Paris.

11 July – General Pétain forms the Vichy government.
France is divided into the Occupied Zone and the
Unoccupied Zone.

17 August – The Germans prohibit Jews who have fled to the
Unoccupied Zone from returning to the Occupied Zone.
*September – Freddie escapes from the camp at St Cyprien and goes
to Gaillac, in the Unoccupied Zone.*

27 September – A German decree is passed requiring a census of
Jews in the Occupied Zone.

3 October – The Vichy government passes the first Statute of
Jews, banning Jews from public service and positions capable
of influencing public opinion.
*November – Freddie leaves Gaillac and goes to occupied Brussels.
December – Freddie arrives in Paris, where he meets the Hubermans
and Otto Geringer.*

1941

*January – Freddie starts works as a 'guide' for German soldiers
visiting the Pigalle district of Paris.*
February – A cinema in Paris shows the antisemitic film
Le Juif Süss (The Jew Süss)

14 May – The first *rafle* of Jews in Paris takes place.

2 June – The Vichy government calls for a census of Jews in the
Unoccupied Zone and excludes Jews from commerce and
industry.

22 July – Vichy legislation authorises the confiscation of Jewish
property.

20 August – The second *rafle* of Jews in Paris takes place.

21 August – A German soldier is killed at Barbès-Rochechouart

Métro station in Paris.

3   September – A German soldier is killed at the Gare de l'Est in Paris.

5   September – The antisemitic exhibition *Le Juif et la France* opens in Paris.

2-3 October – Eugène Deloncle, of the fascist Comité Secret d'Action Révolutionnaire, organises the blowing-up of seven synagogues in Paris.

8   December – The USA and Britain declare war on Japan after the attack on Pearl Harbor of the previous day.

1942

20 January – The Wannsee Conference commits Germany to the 'Final Solution'.

3   March – The first bombing raid by the RAF on France.

27 March – The first trainload of Jews leaves the detention camp at Drancy, in Paris, for Auschwitz.

29 May – Jews in the Occupied Zone are ordered to wear the yellow star.

1   June – Responsibility for security in France is transferred from the German Army to the SS.

16-17 July – The *Grand Rafle* of the Jews of Paris, who are taken to the Vélodrome d'Hiver and then to Drancy for deportation to Auschwitz.

5   August – The first Jews from camps in the Unoccupied Zone are sent to Drancy *en route* to Auschwitz.

13 August – Switzerland closes its border to Jewish refugees.

8   November – Allied forces enter North Africa.

11 November – The Germans capture the Unoccupied Zone.

11 December – The Vichy government orders Jews in the Unoccupied Zone to have their personal documents stamped 'Juif' or 'Juive'.

1943

16 February – Service du Travail Obligatoire (STO), Compulsory Work Service, is introduced in France.

1 March – The demarcation line dividing France is abolished for 'full French nationals'.

9 July – The Allies take Sicily.

July – Freddie is arrested by the Gestapo and warned to cease all contact with German soldiers on Place Pigalle. He leaves Paris and joins the Francs-Tireurs et Partisans Français, part of the Maquis Resistance movement, near Figeac, in the Lot département.

August – Freddie's Resistance group blows up a train.

8 September – The Germans take over Italian-occupied territory in southern France. Italy agrees an armistice with the Allies.

September – Allied troops enter. Freddie is arrested by the Milice (Vichy police) and taken to Drancy.

6 *October – Freddie's name appears on the deportation list at Drancy.*

7 *October – Freddie is deported to Auschwitz, arriving on 10 October.*

1944

6 June – The Allies carry out the D-Day landing in Normandy.

15 August – French and Allied troops land in Provence.

17 August – The last trainload of Jews leaves France for Auschwitz.

25 August – The Free French, under Leclerc, enter Paris with General de Gaulle.

1945

18 January –Auschwitz is evacuated and the prisoners, including Freddie, begin the 'Death March'.

19 January – Freddie arrives at Gleiwitz, in Poland.

249

21-7 January – Freddie is taken by train to Mittelbau-Dora concentration camp, near Nordhausen.

27 January – Soviet troops liberate Auschwitz.
March – Mittelbau-Dora is evacuated and Freddie is taken to Bergen-Belsen.

15 April – Bergen-Belsen is liberated by British troops.

28 April – Freddie returns to Paris and stays at the Hôtel Lutecia.
May – Freddie recuperates at the home of Dr Bennetin in Salornay-sur- Guye, in eastern France, where he is reunited with Eric.
June – Freddie is reunited with Leo and Annie Bodek in Nice, and with his remaining family in Limoges.

1946

January – Freddie is reunited with Otto in Le Havre and holidays with him in Switzerland.
May – Freddie works as an interpreter with the US Army in Limoges.

1947

19 January – Freddie sails from Le Havre to New York, arriving on 29 January, and is reunited with his brothers and other relatives.

1948

March – Freddie moves to Baltimore and begins work with the Standard Textile Company.

1949

9 October – Freddie meets his future wife Freda on a blind date.

24 November – Freddie and Freda become engaged.

31 December – Freddie and Freda are married.

1952

1 July – Freddie and Freda leave the USA to settle in London.

1953

28 April – Marcia Knoller is born

1956

16 June – Susie Knoller is born.

APPENDIX 3

MY PARENTS' REGISTRATION OF THEIR ASSETS AS JEWS

My parents Registration of their assets as Jews . Vienna 1938

254

— 2 —

III. Betriebsvermögen (vgl. Anleitung Ziff. 11 und 12):

a) Wenn Sie am 27. April 1938 Inhaber eines Gewerbebetriebs waren (vgl. Anleitung Ziff 11):

Bezeichnung des Betriebs (Firma), Ort der Geschäftsleitung und Art des Betriebs (z. B. Maschinenfabrik, Lebensmittelhandlung, Gastwirtschaft, Tischlerei)	Gesamtwert des Betriebs nach Abzug der Betriebsschulden RM	Wenn der Betrieb noch Anderen gehörte: Wie hoch war Ihr Anteil? (z. B. 1/2)
1	2	3

Außer den Angaben in den Spalten 1 bis 3 ist die Berechnung des „Gesamtwerts des Betriebs" in einer Anlage im einzelnen zu erläutern.

b) Wenn Sie am 27. April 1938 an offenen Handelsgesellschaften, Kommanditgesellschaften oder ähnlichen Gesellschaften beteiligt waren:

α) Um welche Gesellschaften handelt es sich? (Bezeichnung des Betriebs, Firma, Ort der Geschäftsleitung) ______

β) Wie hoch war Ihr Anteil? ______ Wie hoch war der Wert Ihres Anteils? ______ RM

c) Wenn Sie am 27. April 1938 Vermögen besaßen, das der Ausübung eines freien Berufs diente (vgl. Anleitung Ziff. 12):

α) Art des freien Berufs? ______ (z. B. Augenarzt, Rechtsanwalt, Architekt, Kunstmaler)

β) Wo wurde der Beruf ausgeübt? ______ (Gemeinde, Straße, Hausnummer)

γ) Welchen Wert hatte das dem freien Beruf gewidmete Reinvermögen am 27. April 1938? ______ RM

(Eine Aufstellung dieses Vermögens, aufgegliedert insbesondere nach Inventar (z. B. Instrumente, Bibliothek) und Außenständen, ist beizufügen. Wenn Sie den freien Beruf zusammen mit anderen Personen ausüben, ist in der Aufstellung das gemeinschaftliche Vermögen aufzuführen und der Wert Ihres Anteils hieran anzugeben.)

IV. Sonstiges Vermögen, insbesondere Kapitalvermögen (vgl. Anleitung Ziff. 13 bis 21):

Welchen Wert hatte das Ihnen am 27. April 1938 gehörige sonstige Vermögen (ohne Abzug von Schulden), u. zw.:

a) Festverzinsliche Wertpapiere einschl. Schuldbuchforderungen und Sachwertanleihen (z. B. Anleihen oder Schuldverschreibungen von Staaten und Gemeinden, Obligationen von Industriegesellschaften, Pfandbriefe, Steuergutscheine usw.),

Wertpapiere mit Dividendenertrag (z. B. Aktien, Kuxe und Genußscheine, Reichsbankanteilscheine, Reichsbahnvorzugsaktien),

Geschäftsanteile an inländischen und ausländischen Unternehmen? (z. B. Anteile an Gesellschaften mit beschränkter Haftung. — Name der Gesellschaft, Ort der Geschäftsleitung ist anzugeben) — vgl. Anleitung Ziff. 14 —.

Bezeichnung des Wertpapiers usw. (Wird ein Bankauszug beigefügt, aus dem sich die Angaben zu den Sp. 1 bis 5 vollständig ergeben, so genügt die Ausfüllung der Sp. 5 unter Hinweis auf den Bankauszug)	Zinssatz ¹)	Nennbetrag des gesamten Besitzes an dem in Sp. 1 bezeichneten Wertpapier usw.	Kurswert gemeiner (Verkaufs-) Wert in Prozenten oder für 1 Stück o. dgl.	Wert für den in Sp. 3 angegebenen Nennbetrag RM	Bemerkungen
1	2	3	4	5	6
10 Stück Trifailer Kohle	—	Sfr Kcs 1400.—		96.32	
1 Triefferaul. Los		S 500.—		335.—	
1 Baulos 1926				20.—	

¹) Nur bei festverzinslichen Werten anzugeben, nicht z. B. bei Aktien, Kuxen, Anteilen an Gesellschaften mit beschränkter Haftung.

NOTES

1
The Island of Matzos

1. Ironically, almost a full year after Anschluss, Otto received a letter from the Army, reproduced in this book, which he refers to in a letter to Eric dated 6 February 1939:

> *Today I received an express, registered summons from Army Headquarters regarding recruitment.*

The bureaucratic error was oddly comforting in the circumstances, a memory of a more civilised era. Otto went to the authorities and produced a document dated 6 August 1938, stating that, as a *Volljude* (full-Jew), he was exempt from military service.

2. Recently I obtained these registration forms, completed in my father's excellent hand, from the Austrian archives, The asset form

he completed is actually dated 15 July 1938. The document, reproduced in this book, shows his declaration. Among other items, he lists a life insurance policy with Anker Insurance Company, some shares and savings accounts. He lists a gold tiepin with small diamonds, wedding rings, a gold watch and chain, a lady's gold watch. On 6 August my father was instructed to offer his shares for sale to the Reichsbank. I do not know the terms of this forced sale. He informed the authorities on 11 August that he had offered his shares to the Länderbank for sale.

3. On 6 December 1938 my father wrote a postcard to Eric, who was in Rotterdam waiting to embark for America:

Dearest Erich
For your departure tomorrow I wish you, from your dear mother, from Otto and myself a wonderful and safe crossing. When you arrive in New York, please send me a telegram. Make sure that your trunk No. EK 100 has been properly loaded. The lining of your coat will arrive, with luck, tomorrow. We will be thinking of you tomorrow on your departure. We are, thank God, in good health and we have only one wish, to hear good news from you and Fredy...

My father's reference to the lining of the coat almost certainly indicates that small valuables were secreted there.

2
The Lost Coin

1. Otto wrote to Eric on 19 December 1938, on behalf of himself and our parents:

...thank God you have arrived safely in America. I have

very important requests for you: 1) When is a son able to get his parents to the States notwithstanding the quota? Does he have to be over twenty-one or not? How long would he have had to be living in the country? Can he borrow the necessary bank deposit? 2) In the case of a Jewish musician (meaning myself) entering into a contract, can he then enter the States through this despite the quota? Would a contract from a private club suffice? Perhaps you can send me some sheet music of a new popular song.

I was in Holland for ten days and have been through terrible times ... tell Mr Apte about the dangerous position I am in, and that I have tried everything to get away from here, but that unfortunately I have not succeeded. Tell him also that as far as I am concerned I could not care less where I go, perhaps he can get me a permit for England? The most important thing would be an affidavit, then I could leave in May 1939. Please try your best. It is very hot for me here.

Otto was fortunate to escape with his life. He set the story out in a letter dated 20 April 1985 to his friend and fellow escapee Norbert Fuchs, who had emigrated to Australia:

Dear Norbert
Not knowing your history for the past forty years does not diminish the excitement to hear of the wedding of your daughter. I do hope that you will write to me with your life story. I reach on 5 April 1985 my 72nd year, 'nicht schlecht' [not bad], as one says in Viennese. I am still working 8–10 hours per day. I am sure you have read in the newspapers about the Holocaust celebrations in the States, especially in

259

Washington DC. It is therefore quite fitting to think back on the night of December... 1938, when you and I approached the German Dutch border near Venlo. I recall a lot of snow, coldness, howling of dogs and suddenly you were out of sight. I succeeded in crossing the border, was accepted by recommendation to a Dutch Jewish family, but two days later was jailed by Dutch police in Amsterdam. After a few days I was transported back to the German border and with another thirty refugees we walked through the No Man's Land to the border of Germany. I separated myself from the group and spent a few hours at the 'Strassengraben' [ditch] shaving myself in order to look better. At 6.00am I arrived at the German border and was told that about one hour prior to my arrival the SS were waiting for all of us and took all the people to concentration camps. With luck I was able to contact my parents in Vienna and returned by train to Austria...

In his interview for the Spielberg Archive, interviews conducted with survivors of Nazi persecution, Otto adds something significant about his delay at the ditch. He says, 'I do not know why I did what I did, but I thought it would be much too dangerous to go with the group to the border.'

On January 3 1939 my father wrote to Eric:

We received your dear letter of 21st of last month today. In fact, the very first letter from Miami. We enjoyed reading the details, but especially that you have started working. May God grant that your sponsor is satisfied with your efforts. Dear Erich! Have you visited Tanty Fanny Feldherr in New York? I hope so. Dear Otto is already home again as a 'flying Dutchman'. What he suffered in Holland cannot be described. It would be such a blessing for him and us if we could legally get to America, provided he could get an affidavit. I am sure, dear Erich, that you will do your utmost to get Otto and Fredy to America. Have you asked our relatives in New York whether they can do this for both of them? Otto's case is the most urgent, because young people cannot stay here. Dear Fredy's situation is middling, he misses us very much. He is not working and is not allowed to, and this is the worst thing for a young man. Jos Apte helps him unstintingly and invites him for daily supper. What a wonderful person! May God grant that our children have the luck to meet only good human beings. We pray to God every day to keep our patrons and protectors in good health and to grant them god fortune. Amen!

Dear Erich! We are going to write to you once a week on Tuesdays. Please promise to do the same and write to us each week, then we will receive post from you once a week. You cannot begin to imagine how we look forward to hearing from you. Please also write to dear Fredy, which he would love. His address is: Alfred Knoller, Antwerpen, Belgien, Statiestraat 36.

I am going to send you a few of our things, which you can look after for us. Tell us to which address to send these. I am looking forward to receiving your next letter soon.

2. I am guided as to the date by my mother's letter to Eric of 17 January 1939, in which she asks him: 'Did Fredy write to you that he has received his cello?'

3. Eric's birthday was 11 March, the date of the Anschluss. My parents wrote to him on 5 March 1939, sending him birthday greetings, but in a bitter-sweet way. Things had changed for my father:

Dearest Erich

We have today received your dear letter of 22nd February. 'First of all, I wish you on your birthday on 11th March very much happiness and health.' As you can see, dear Erich, I already know some English – yes, 11th March is for all of us a memorable day because on this day our destiny has been sealed … may God grant us the opportunity to see each other soon with joy. Amen. I would have liked to have bought you something for your birthday but unfortunately we are too far away from each other. Dearest Erich, as far as our affidavit is concerned it would give us great pleasure if only Mr Apte would give us the affidavit, not your boss. Because the Aptes are already known at this consulate. Also, remember that Mr Bill [Apte] promised to do something for us. Mr Meyer has already received his affidavit from the Aptes. In the meantime he will go to England. I am jealous of Mr Apte… I have already left my job at Grossner & Weiss because the firm has now been 'Aryanised' and they now have a Christian bookkeeper, who has been there since December. Otto is trying very hard to get to England in order to wait there whilst his affidavits are completed. He needs someone there to sponsor him. I would also like Fredy to go there, but he also needs a sponsor, as Mundy Sperber did … please be careful when you are driving a car. You will receive the little case, you will have to pay the freight Tampa–Miami, but nothing more. The typewriter is locked. On the right of the machine is a button which locks it. Do not force it or you will break it. I will send you the manual so you can see how to use it, in case you want to write…

Aunt Fanny Feldherr wrote to us that she ought to receive a letter from you. I beg you to write to her because she is the only one who has a good heart as she wanted to do something for us if only she had the possibility. Her address is … 1036, Bryant Avenue, New York…

How sadly this reads. My father must have written to many other relatives, and this letter demonstrates their reaction, which would seem to have been silence.

Included were letters from my mother and Otto. My mother wrote:

My dearest Erichl, I am filled with joy through your letters, this is the only joy one has today ... today is Purim. One should be happy. It does not make sense. You, my dear child, take care of yourself...

You know that coming to the USA is not so easy for us, it seems the Vienna quota has been closed for two months and Fredy yearns to get away from Antwerp. It is not so easy. It would be wonderful to receive 2 permits so that Otto and Fredy could go to England.

For several months my father had not told Eric that he had lost his job in December, although he had written several letters to him in between. Perhaps he said nothing because he would have had to train the new bookkeeper, so he probably remained until January or February 1939. Or perhaps, quite simply, he did not want to worry Eric, but then felt he had to share this blow. I knew of my father's situation through letters he wrote to me in Belgium.

Meanwhile my parents were able to tell Eric that Otto's departure was imminent:

April 5 1939
...thank God you are well. We have received your letter. We hope you will succeed in sending the missing documents for Otto. We

263

cannot use these documents for Fredy because they are in Otto's name... We hear good things about you in a letter from Dr Georg Jänner... Be happy that you are where you are... What a joy it would be to see how you look... Otto will shortly go temporarily to England. And when his affidavit is completed he will then leave for America. Do you think, dear Eric, that we also will soon receive an affidavit? Just in case, please write down our dates of birth: David Knoller born 3 January 1882 in Dynov, Poland

Marie Knoller born 5 August 1885 in Lemberg, Poland.

The reference to 'missing documents' is to a consular examination, which would either have been a documentary one or perhaps a health check.

In a further letter to Eric of April 1939 my mother's despair breaks through:

...Fredy writes to us now every second day. He wrote to us that you have no reason to be upset with him. He wrote to you on the 2nd and has sent you birthday wishes, and has thanked you for his affidavit. So peace... The Neufelds have left for Berlin, then Belgium, afterwards to London and then Australia. Lucky people! Anny Morgenstern and Mr Lastinger had their examination and will also leave soon. Hans Herr leaves also, soon we will be the last Jews in Austria...

The reference to Eric's being 'upset with him' concerns his disappointment that I had not wished him a happy birthday. The reference to an affidavit concerns my affidavit for America. As with Otto's affidavit, there were certain other formalities to be gone through to finalise my emigration. The invasion of Belgium and my flight into France ended these hopes at that stage. It can only be a matter of speculation whether, if I had remained in Austria I might have managed to finalise my papers and avoid what lay ahead for me.

In May 1939, after entering Holland again, now legally with affidavit in order, Otto left for England. His letter of 20 April 1985 to Norbert Fuchs continues:

...through some contacts of my father [who worked in the Kultusgemeinde] I was able to join many hundreds of young Viennese fellows and travel to Kent, England, into the famous 'Kitchener Refugee Camp', where I spent a full year until April 1940. During the year I formed an orchestra in the camp, became its pianist and conductor, gave many concerts throughout England for the Military Auxiliary Pioneer Corps...

4. Letter of 22 October 1939 from my mother to Eric:

Dear Erich
I wrote to you yesterday but today I must tell you that I have received the following letter from the consulate in Vienna:

David, Marie and Alfred Knoller,
Following your completed form No. 41 we have to inform you that we have thoroughly investigated your case. We were unable to find any proof that you registered in spring 1938. You are therefore not registered at the time given by you and we would advise you to complete the attached questionnaire, and return it to us...

You can imagine the anger and frustration. We are desperate and do not know what to do… There is no doubt, we know we registered together… What a misfortune. We have written to Mr D. Apte, asking for his advice.

Our only hope was that we would soon be together with our children… Can you imagine when it would be our turn if we registered again? Can one live here that long?… This is a question of life or death. Mr Simpson should do all in his power to see that the complaint gets to Washington without delay. There should be no question of expenses, one should even engage a lawyer.

My eyes hurt from crying. How can one live without having any hope of being together with our children?

5. A letter to Eric from my father three days later repeats the self-censorship of the one I received, and also mentioned the small hope offered by his official position at the Jewish Community Centre:

25 October 1939
Many are forced are going to the country where I was born (Viele müssen sollen in das Land gehen wo ich geboren bin), but for the moment I am exempt because I am a public functionary.

6. I do not know what happened to anyone else from Eksaarde, save for my cousin Maxl. Maxl had ended up in a group of refugees heading for Ostend, hoping to get a boat to England. The brave German catholic led this group. They got as far as Middelkirk, where they were halted by the gendarmes and housed in some army barracks. At some point in all this confusion the brave Catholic disappeared. With the arrival of the Germans a day later the Belgian gendarmes presented their conquerors with the refugees. Jews were never mentioned. The

Germans, like the Belgians before them, did not ask anyone for identification though, of course, the Jewish refugees from Eksaarde had their passports with the large red 'J' stamped on them. Maxl had no passport at all, only his Swiss birth certificate. The Germans politely asked the group where they wanted to go. Maxl and many others said they wanted to go to Brussels so the Germans put them on a train. Maxl then made his way to the Jewish Community Centre. From here Maxl returned to the house in Brussels which he had shared with his family, only to find that they had abandoned it. Neighbours told him that the whole household had fled, saying they wanted to get to France. Maxl found his sewing machine intact, and found work.

3
Weathering the Storm

1. My parents' postcard to Eric confirms that I had written to them shortly before 20 July 1940, the date of their postcard to him. They wrote again to him on 5 August:

> *We have received two cards from Fredl in St Cyprien, and even a letter. He tells us that he is in good health and not short of anything. He says he gets plenty of food. Also Uncle and Leo are there. Aunt Genya lives near Toulouse. Fredy asks us to write to him Post Restante Toulouse. I ask you, dear Erich, write to dear Fredy that we are well but temporarily unable to write to him [because of the uncompleted peace negotiations between France and Germany]. Tell him that Maxl remained in Brussels and is well and earns well. I have already written to Maxl that his parents are well.*

2. These community centres were later used by the Germans for the registration and deportation of Jews.

3. Postcard of 10 December 1940 from my father to Eric:

Thank God we are in good health and we hope to hear the same from you. Unfortunately we have not heard from you for months. The waiting wrecks our nerves. I have written to you that Fredy has gone back to Brussels. He wrote to us that all his clothes and laundry and cello have disappeared. Who knows if the poor boy has something warm to put on in Winter. He wants to come back to his native town, however that is not possible.

The last sentence is witness to my homesickness, but what I had written to prompt it is lost for ever, and it is the sad irony of this story that the written words of my parents live on, while those of myself and my brothers, who survived, have been destroyed. Today I cannot even recall the feelings behind my reported words.

4
Escorting the Enemy

1. The last dated letter my parents wrote was to my brother Eric, on 8 January 1941. There was one further one, undated, and this absence of a date, given my father's meticulous nature, is a significant indication of his state of mind.

2. The brothel at 122 Rue de Provence later became off limits to the occupying forces.

6
Drancy

1. I had no idea of the system at first, but at Drancy, as in the ghettos and the concentration camps, internal administration and discipline were in the hands of prisoners designated *Membres de Service* (MS) by the Germans. A few SS officers – just four was

deemed to be the appropriate number at Drancy – directed the MS at the camp. Under this system the Chef de Camp was a Jew, one George Kohn, who controlled a group of thirty men who were in charge of discipline. These men were exempt from the lists for deportation to the East – until such time as they displeased the Germans – so they willingly carried out any orders. The French police, under the command of ex-commissioner of police Guibert, liaised with Kohn and the MS.

Another official at Drancy was a civilian named Fonseque. I believe he was attached to the Vichy government. These men were merely faces at the time and it was only when I began my research after the war that I discovered their names. It was in July 1943, three months before I arrived, that the Germans assumed overall command at Drancy.

2. 'The Boxer' was the nickname of SS *Hauptsturmführer* Brückler, second in command at Drancy. Like the Commandant, Brunner, he was renowned for his harshness and brutality. Another German officer at the camp known for his cruelty was SS *Oberscharführer* Weisel. Incongruously a hairdresser in civilian life, he was more intelligent than Brückler, but quite willing to back up the latter's violence with a stick.

3. The station was that of Bobigny, not far from Drancy. Here prisoners from the camp were assembled in rows of five across and twenty deep. The mathematics was always neat and simple. There were usually one thousand names on each list and ten wagons in each transport, each to carry one hundred people.

The official documentation regarding my particular transport, Convoy 60, was compiled by the French historian Serge Klarsfeld:

'CONVOY 60, OCTOBER 7, 1943

On September 30, Brunner telexed Eichmann and asked him for the go ahead for the departure of a convoy on October 7(XLIX-49). Eichmann responded favourably (XLIX-50) and added that a commando from Stuttgart would arrive to escort the convoy. Convoy 60 included 564 males and 436 females, 108 were children under 18. Among the families were Erna Koch and her two babies, Monique (1) and Nicole, who had just been born on July 22. Herta Bolz with an infant, Henry (2 months) and Elise (3). Others included: Victoria Bovetis and her five children – Maurice (14), Michel (12), Suzanne (10), Simone (8) and Jacqueline (6). There was Raymond Chorezyk (17) his brother, Marcel (16) and their sister, Huguette (11); Annie Feder (3); Simon Friedmann (8); Jean Frydman; Bernard (12) and Irene Garfunkel (7); Colette Goldstein (3); Simon Horyn (1); Raymond Levy (3); Marce Rosenberg (10 months); Camille Sayagh and her five children – Reine (10), Henry (8), Claude (4), Georges (2) and Nicole (10)

This routine telex, No: XLIX-52, was signed by Rothke. It established that in October 7 at 10.30am a convoy of 1000 Jews left Paris-Bobigny with the Meister der Schupo, Schlamm, head of the escort. On October 13, Höss, Commandant of Auschwitz, telexed to Rothke telex No: XLIX-53, that on October 10th, at 05.30, the convoy actually arrived.

When they arrived at Auschwitz, 340 men were selected and went to Buna, the I.G. Farben synthetic rubber plant at Auschwitz. They were assigned numbers 156940 to 157279. One hundred and sixty-nine women remained alive and were given numbers 64711 to 64879. The remainder were gassed. In 1945, less than two years later, 31 of the 509 selected survived. Two of the survivors were women.'

4. The new arrivals' goods represented rich pickings on the camp's black market for these privileged inmates.

7
Pitchipoi

1. Schwarz served at the concentration camps of Mauthausen 1939–41, Oranienburg 1941, Auschwitz-Monowitz 1941-5 and then at Natzwiller (in Alsace). He was executed on 20 March 1947.

2. Perez was shot by the SS and died in the arms of a French comrade on the death march to Belsen, which is described in Chapter 8.

3. The Hungarians were among the last racial group to be deported, arriving at Auschwitz in the early summer of 1944. Therefore Imre would have been a relative newcomer, inexperienced in the ways of the camp. I had been at Auschwitz more than a year by this time.

8
Death March

1. Later I learnt that Mittelbau-Dora, or Dora as we called it, was below the Harz mountains, near Buchenwald concentration camp. One of Buchenwald's satellite camps, Mittelbau-Dora produced the V1 and V2 rockets.

9
Vive la Vie

1. Leo's parents were of Polish origin and, although they lived in Vienna, did not take Austrian citizenship. Had Leo remained in Austria until he was twenty-one, citizenship would have been automatically conferred on him and, with it, the obligation to undertake military service.